BOURNEMOUTH FIREMEN AT WAR

Ted Hughes

Dorset Publishing Company dpx
at the WINCANTON PRESS
National School, North Street, Wincanton, Somerset BA9 9AT

ISBN (International Standard Book Number) 0 948699 09 4

Publishing details. First published 1991. Text copyright E.R. ("Ted") Hughes © 1991. Photographs copyright the various photographers and copyright owners. Captions copyright Rodney Legg © 1991.

Printing credits. Typeset by Reg Ward at Holwell, Dorset, and output by Wordstream Limited of Poole. Layout by Rodney Legg at Wincanton Press, Somerset. Printed in Great Britain at The Alden Press, Oxford.

WARFARE ON SUNDAY

FULL STORY OF LIGHTNING RAID

Images of war: ruins of the Central Hotel and Punshon Memorial Church, Richmond Hill (opposite) and J.E.Beale Limited (above, photograph courtesy Mr Nigel Beale), after Bournemouth's worst air raid, 23 May 1943.

CONTENTS

Ted Hughes: remembering Bournemouth at war.

Foreword

I believe there would be little disagreement that the image and ways of a Fire Brigade should be fully modern and up-to-date, using the latest in technology, equipment and premises. Firemen are forever keen to find new techniques and methods and anything which can improve the efficiency of firefighting and rescue. With this concentration on being up-to-date and looking to the future, it might be thought that within the service there is relatively little interest in Fire Brigade history. Nothing could be further from the truth. What we can do today and where we go tomorrow depends in large measure on what happened yesterday.

Ted Hughes's book will be greatly appreciated, not only by those who share memories of the last war and preceding years, but by a far wider and younger readership. Many of those who survived the war years encountered dangers and difficulties in times which were dramatic and demanding. At the same time, life was exciting and absorbing.

Like so many of us, Ted Hughes did not set out to be a fireman, but became involved with the Fire Brigade only to discover that it was an institution full of interest with a certain something that made it rather special. Even after the passage of many years following retirement, his feelings are shown not to have changed.

The author of this book is to be greatly commended for the extensive efforts he has made in recording valuable information and setting it down for posterity. He has, however, done more than some others who have written such histories. By focusing events on his personal experiences from the age of 16, he has managed to paint a very vivid picture of what the life of a fireman was like in those early days.

Together with Ted Hughes and many others, I am pleased to have found and made a career of the Fire Service with all its traditions and developments over so many generations.

As the present Chief Fire Officer with responsibility for the fire protection of Bournemouth, I am privileged to be asked to write the foreword for this book. I recommend it to all its future readers and trust that amongst other things it will encourage serving firemen to discharge their duty with the same professionalism as our predecessors.

T. BASSETT
Chief Fire Officer
Dorset Fire Brigade.

Ted Hughes: four years in the service, at the age of 20, in 1933.

Introduction

The last thing on earth that I ever contemplated when finally discarding my uniform on 31 March 1964, after nearly 35 years' service, was to be further concerned with fire brigade affairs, much less to spend a couple of years nearly a quarter of a century later not only writing history but having to re-live a period of life which at that time appeared to be entirely concluded.

This is the second part of a tripartite work which has been preceded by "The Volunteers", being the story of the early Bournemouth Fire Brigade [1870-1929] to be followed by "The Post-War B.F.B.", yet to be published. The original title of this present volume was "The Professionals", for the 1930s saw not only the termination of the volunteer era but the advent of such growth by a whole-time and well-equipped establishment as earned us the reputation of being one of the leading brigades in the country. I felt that the World War Two story of the Brigade needed to be introduced some ten years prior to September 1939 in order to present not only a picture of pre-war conditions but also of our build-up to the situation in which our first professional chief fire officer, W.H.Barker, with appropriate timing, took over in April 1938. Nor should it be overlooked that during those vital ten years much concentrated thought was being given in Whitehall and elsewhere to the real possibility of extensive fire-blitz conditions.

This brief part of my narrative is confined largely to the activities of the Bournemouth Fire Brigade and the Auxiliary Fire Service which it produced before being overcome, if not devoured, by the National Fire Service in August 1941. It would not be immodest to claim that throughout the quite extraordinary and dramatic period following April 1938, a virtually unrecognised handful of Bournemouth professional firemen, working day and night, produced what turned out to be a model for the whole nation of fire service vigilance. In our town's centenary year, may it be so recorded.

Some part at least of this story involved uncovering my own memories and removing the dust from diaries and personal records, but in the main, the telling of the stories offered in this book has been made possible by the work and diligence of others and the splendid co-operation of old friends and new acquaintances who have readily given encouragement during the many months of essential research in pursuit of distant material.

7

I extend my grateful thanks to Michael Edgington of the Lansdowne Central Reference Library, who originally suggested that a work such as this was needed for local record, and who, with his most obliging staff, has kindly and freely provided access to the treasury of records so expertly maintained under his care.

Convinced that the Fire Service itself would relish the results of my work, Station Officer Simon Adamson has given me constant encouragement, and has allowed me access to his own mine of Service information and supplied essential literature. Quite a number of Fire Service "old-timers" have racked their memories and have not complained at my numerous and sometimes unexpected calls upon them. Names are not listed lest some be overlooked, the exceptions being Mr Keith Buchanan who, in the course of his research and writing of ex-Mayor Harry Mears's life story shared the latter's wartime reminiscences. Thanks are also due to retired Divisional Commander "Rocky" Robinson, whose bookshelf was lightened from time to time; and to a very old friend and colleague, Dick Law, who has checked quite a few facts by virtue of his own long and wide experience, and who has given aid throughout periods of a writer's weariness.

The reader is asked to forgive repetition, or autobiographic tendencies that were perhaps inevitable when resurrecting memories of events in which the writer was personally involved. As for the detail contained herein, it is but fractional, so as not to overcrowd with statistics, however relevant, what is intended to be a record of noteworthy happenings, to be read with enjoyment.

E.R.H.

The author thanks Bournemouth Borough Council for allowing him full access to its records. Other factual data from the files of Bournemouth Echo and Bournemouth Times, and from 'The History of the British Fire Service', by G.V. Blackstone,CBE, GM.

This book is dedicated to the Firemen of Bournemouth, whose courage and service continue through war and peace.

A new kind of service

On 23 May 1929, a clerk was appointed to the staff of the Bournemouth Fire Brigade. It was on 30 May, as a rather frail, skinny and very nervous 16-year-old, recently emerged from seven years' sheltered yet extremely harsh schooling at the Royal Orphanage, Wolverhampton, that I entered the side door of the two-bay Central Fire Station, Holdenhurst Road. It was a world of adults, and my first sight of either fire station or engine. Firemen in overalls and round caps looked across in amusement as they sang lustily to the rhythm of their brass-polishing and a diminuendo followed the gruff intervention of veteran Station Officer Albert Cook as he ushered me into the office. Mr Cook, a small, somewhat tubby man, moustached and wearing undress uniform with brass buttons and shining full-shoulder epaulets, undoubtedly felt as embarrassed as the newcomer as he pointed to the newly-constructed shelf-type desk and stool reminiscent of David Copperfield's apprentice-ship. In addition, there stood in that small office Mr Cook's own desk, a stationery cupboard, a plug-type switchboard, and on the wall a bell-control board bearing individual push-buttons, switches and names, dominated by a glass-enclosed pendulum, the conveyor of fire calls.

The administration was to involve all manner of ancillary tasks. The wages of the twelve-man staff had to be prepared, the ordering of material, invoicing, the preparation of reports, all correspondence and such typing as could be manipulated on the most archaic machine, with a double set of keys and a hideous purple ribbon, which the local museum would have liked as a historical exhibit. In addition, there was an exercise which remained a custom throughout the Service for far too many years — the time-consuming, boring and inconsequential logging of fire station comings and goings. A course of Sloan-Duployan shorthand over the following months, though useful to the user, proved throughout the years the incompetence of those who would dictate. My salary was £1 per week, rising to £1 5s in April 1931, £1 10s in February 1933 and £2 in October 1933. Hours of duty were 8 a.m. to 6 p.m. from Monday to Friday, and 8 a.m. to 1 p.m. on Saturday.

Captain Harry Wall, the last of the volunteer chief officers, administered the mixed volunteer/professional brigade from his home at 19, Portman Road, Boscombe, where he conducted his business as undertaker and small builder. He had taken office upon the retirement of Captain Henry Robson, a well-known

Bournemouth grocer and ex-Mayor, in 1921. Captain Wall had joined the Brigade in January 1902, being promoted to Senior Fireman in 1905, a Foreman in 1908 and Third Officer in May 1916. With his waxed moustache, he appeared to be somewhat stern but in fact he was a quiet and most understanding gentleman.

Fire Brigade clerical administration was an innovation in what amounted to a new type of service. Any permanent addition to expenditure was seen as a particularly unpalatable exercise, for the "Cinderella Service", as it was to be known for many years to come, was non-profitmaking in the eyes of local councils, and Bournemouth, although it was a little more progressive than many others, was not exempt from this attitude. Captain Wall made every reasonable effort to win for his clerk inclusion into the Local Authority's A.P.T. (Administrative, Professional and Technical) grading. His endeavours were in vain, and the virtually inevitable alternative, bearing in mind the dismal unemployment levels and the clerk's family predicament, became absorption into operational involvement in addition to his administrative responsibility. This was effected from 6 November 1934 and I, far from my own intention, became Fireman-Clerk − jacta alea est!

Exploration of the Central Fire Station on that first bright May morning had revealed, immediately outside the office door, the 85-feet turntable ladders by Merryweather − boldly named "the Robson" − and beyond the brass-emblazoned Dennis Pump. "The Engine Room", as it was then called, sparkled with its floor well scrubbed in the regular Saturday morning routine, and its gleaming brown-tiled walls topped by a frieze which, in plaster, depicted fire engines from the earliest to the one proudly displayed at the opening of the station in August 1902. This Bournemouth frieze has remained unique within the Service.

A door leading off the engine room revealed a narrow stairway leading downwards to a stokehold and a wide, bending staircase up to the first floor, which consisted of a billiards room facing Holdenhurst Road and the Brigade Engineer's married quarters to the rear. The second floor had the Station Officer's married quarters on both sides of a centre corridor, and above this, the roof space contained a small turret room which still remains undisturbed.

Facing astern from the engine room, the once well-occupied stables were to the left, a workshop and outer-toilet to the right and the yard between, bridged by a glass roof. Following the

10

right outer extremity of the station, a wall divided the drill yard from a privately-owned apple orchard. At the far end of the yard stood the boundary wall of the Hotel Woodville, the grounds of which extended to Christchurch Road. On the Cotlands Road side of the yard were numbers 4 to 14 Cotlands Road, which were privately-owned boarding houses. Each consisted of a basement, ground floor, and two upper floors. Their gardens and three feet walls afforded excellent facilities for visitors wishing to view fire-drills, or otherwise to contact young and handsome firemen. Just so did Fireman Wally Churchill come to marry his holiday girl. The three-storey high tower, with its fine domed top and engine-and-horses weathervane, dominated the drill yard.

Apart from Station Officer Cook and Ken Devereux, the Brigade's ex-Wolseley-indentured Engineer, the professional staff at the Central Fire Station comprised Joe Thackwray (painter and signwriter), Reg "Connie" Wyeth (painter and decorator), Alf Brooke (electrician), Bert Hutchins (carpenter) and Frank Barker (bricklayer). Firemen Thackwray, Wyeth and Brooke, being single men, slept rather roughly in either the former stables, part of which were then used as the carpenter's shop, or in the roof space. They were, as the other single men who were later enrolled, well victualled with motherly care by Mrs Cook. Fireman Hutchins retired to his married quarters at Winton Fire Station each night, as did Fireman Barker to his single billet at Westhill Road. Frank Barker later married Edith, the younger daughter of Westhill's Station Fireman Jack Mullins. Fireman Ted "Taffy" Williams resided with his family at Winton Fire Station. At Pokesdown Station dwelt Fireman Joe Frampton and Fireman Bill Baker, with their families.

The pay of the married men at the sub-stations was £3.16s per week (reckoned for superannuation purposes) with emoluments of free fuel and light but with a deduction of 18s per week for rent. Single men received £3.10s per week, the 10s paid in lieu of proper quarters. Superannuation deductions were at the rate of 5 percent of the gross wage, and National Health contributions were 1s.2d per week. Sick pay was limited to three weeks of full pay followed by six weeks of half-pay, Health Insurance payments being deducted. Accident pay was limited to whatever the Council deemed appropriate under the Workmen's Compensation Regulations, which did not differentiate between a fireman and any other Corporation workman. Leave was limited to a period of sixteen hours (7 a.m. to 11 p.m.) every eighth day, so that a week's duty averaged 154 hours.

Life in 1929 was somewhat different from that of the present day, with its dominance of turbulent possessiveness. There was less attention to political wiles and manipulations and greater adherence to post-world war hopes; and the weekly soothing dream-romance of the silver screen provided contentment in fantasy to limit aspirations and preserve the hopefully unchanging present. A kind of naïveté characterised official and commercial manoeuvrings, with far less of the blatantly mind-twisting propaganda which affronts the intellect today. Although life in the South was comparatively quiet and comfortable, the writer's still vivid memory is of the appalling poverty which then plagued the North and Midlands – the haggard faces, bare feet and unconquered tuberculosis of the people beset by mass unemployment.

But the life of a fireman in Bournemouth was not so bad, even with restricted freedom. On every slight breeze was borne to him the scent of Bournemouth's pines, then in rich abundance. For his off-duty days he could buy a good bicycle for £4 19s 6d (Humber, Rudge, Enfield) or a new motor-cycle for £75, or even a Morris Cowley saloon car for £190, with top grade petrol at 1s 6d per gallon (Shell, Pratts) or low grade at 9d. A new three-piece suit for £2 10s could be bought from the Fifty Shilling Tailors in the Square, or one made-to-measure from Burtons at £2 15s, plus a shirt at 5s 11d. He could take a return trip to London with a Shamrock and Rambler's coach for 12s 6d, or for his 14 days' annual leave he could buy a cabin suitcase for 2s 6d and enjoy a week's tour of Paris for £6 6s. Untroubled by scare of lung cancer, he could buy five Wills Gold Flake cigarettes for 3d, or a tin of 50 Players for 2s 6d, and a pint of beer for 8d. As for food, a large loaf cost 4d. Per pound butter cost 1s, sugar 3d, tea from 1s, cheese 1s 4d, and a pound pot of Robinson's "Golden Shred" marmalade was 9d. On getting married, he could buy a good quality three-piece lounge suite (from Bright's, no less!) for £4 15s and a complete bedroom suite for £24 3s.

The Brigade's uniform at this time was of excellent quality, supplied with regularity by Messrs Huggins of Bristol. Fire tunics and fire trousers were of thick and almost waterproof melton cloth. Leggings were not then issued. Fire boots were from Adams Bros. (Raunds), and of the best leather, as were the elastic-sided (later metal-clipped) day boots. Undress jackets were of fine serge and fitted to the neck, and the caps of the traditional fore-and-aft type. Buttons and badges bore the NFBA insignia. Brass helmets continued to be worn until replaced, for fires and drills, by Glasgow-pattern leather helmets as supplied by Charles Winn and Company at £2 6s in November 1930. Brass helmets, which required eternal cleaning and taking apart for every such occasion, were accompanied by the wearing of white gloves for ceremonial parades until November 1938. The specially strengthened leather belts were equipped not only with axe-pouches bearing wooden-handled axes, but each with a heavy spring-loaded chrome hook with brass belt clip.

The following were Bournemouth's appliances in 1929: At Central, a Dennis Pump (EL 4410) and a Merryweather 85 feet wooden Turntable Ladder. At Pokesdown, a Dennis Tender Escape Carrier (EL 2343). At Westhill Road, a Dennis Tender Escape Carrier (EL 4872) and a Leon-Bollee Escape Carrier (EL2151). At Winton, a Dennis Tender Escape Carrier (RU 5665).

These machines had served the best of their days and a special mention must be made of the truly heroic feats of engineering which Engineer Ken Devereux conducted in order to keep them on the run. Often with parts made up at the Borough Engineer's blacksmiths' workshop at the East Yard or by rushing up to the works of Dennis Bros. at Guildford, using his own tools and expertise, sometimes working through the night and with only a glass roof for shelter, his work of maintenance and his sheer dedication, though unsung, was magnificent. Relief came gradually to his aid. Arising out of the disposal of Pokesdown's Morris Pump following the tragic accident of 26 January 1929, when Volunteer Foreman Giles and Volunteer Fireman Watts were killed at St Catherine's Road, Southbourne, tenders for a replacement were received from Dennis Bros., Leylands and Merryweathers and on 28 October 1929 Dennis's latest 60/70 horsepower Pump (£1,050) complete with its first aid (hose-reel) equipment and a 35 feet extension ladder was delivered (Reg. No. LJ 580). The other Dennis Pump (EL 4410) was transferred to Pokesdown. This was to be the last of the "Braidwood Bodies" in Bournemouth. On 3 April 1930, Arthur Hatton arrived after some years serving as a volunteer in the Aldershot Brigade and promptly donned his overalls with Devereux who was finally consoled by the erection of a fine workshop, complete with tackle and pit, in 1934 (costing £1,300) and a lathe in February 1935.

All appliances, except the latest Dennis Pump, still had their original solid tyres and were without windscreens. A programme proceeded through 1936-7, via the Dunlop Rubber Co. and the adroitness of the Brigade Carpenter — Peter Dorey who

13

had succeeded Bert Hutchins in April 1930 — and this modernisation was achieved. Performance on the road, especially in wet weather, was much improved as also were comfort and safety. The only appliance to retain solid tyres was the Turntable Ladder.

The open "Braidwood Body" was named after James Braidwood, the original "Master of Fire Engines" of the Edinburgh Fire Engine Establishment (1824) who in 1833 became Chief of the London Fire Engine Establishment and stamped the first mark of a professional Fire Service upon the country. Riding this appliance was always something of a hazardous exercise. Its structure was hereditary, from Braidwood's early horse-drawn manuals. A quick turn-out meant inevitably dressing or part-dressing in fire-kit en route to an incident whilst sitting or half-sitting on the open sides of the appliance, hooking one arm around a brass rail. Hopefully, with helmet flopping on head, one would get fire boots on and one arm in tunic before swerving out of the appliance room doors. The driver was not concerned with checking his crew or his own state of dress, and did not attempt to drive in fire boots. Door rope pulled, doors crashed open, foot well down on the accelerator and away it went — with the front man, himself half-dressed, furiously clanging the bell. Day turn-out time was 30 to 60 seconds. At night, the time was within two minutes.

Items of uniform were known to fall off as the machine swerved through traffic along the road. I recall one of my boots flying off on the approach to Boscombe Hill and the driver of a car stopping to pick it up before tearing along behind us whilst his passenger invitingly proffered the boot from the side window. The legs of one's fire trousers were turned with two folds and worn over the fire boots, and again I recall only too vividly, in 1935, taking rather a late leap on to the rear of the departing appliance (LJ 580 — known as "The Flyer") and falling backwards whilst the trouser fold caught in the nozzle of the nearside fire extinguisher. I was dragged on my back down Holdenhurst Road from the Central Fire Station before being deposited at The Lansdowne. The fire bell was clanging and the rest of the crew were unaware of my predicament. That time I returned to the Station, rode my bicycle to the fire, and returned during "make-up" without the often irascible Station Officer Cook ever being aware of the incident.

Stowage of the "Braidwood Body" appliances was somewhat limited in contrast to modern machines. Special cupboards were constructed to house the Siebe Gorman one-hour Proto and

14

half-hour Salvus breathing apparatus. The former replaced the old "diver's helmet" type in 1925. The majority of the other equipment was contained in the side platform boxes. In the centre compartment, above the 40 gallon water tank, the hose was stored, originally as traditional coils but later ribboned and so coupled up that it could be run out straight from the appliance. Two-gallon foam and soda-acid fire extinguishers were carried on the sides and rear and pompier ladders were lashed on the top of either escapes or extension ladders.

Branches, nozzles, breechings, instantaneous couplings and standpipes were always of the heaviest brass and purchased mainly from Charles Winn and Company of Birmingham. We envied the light metal equipment of Germany and Switzerland. Hose, both lined and unlined, was 2¾ inches diameter, and 1929 saw the ordering from MacGregors of 9,600 feet of rubber-lined hose. In 1930, 1,700 feet of canvas hose was sold and replaced again with rubber-lined hose. Westhill's appliances carried standpipe adaptors, from Bournemouth's lug-type to Poole's Surelock variety, and by an arrangement made with Poole Brigade in 1930, all appliances carried V-thread standpipes for use with the Bournemouth Gas and Water Company's flushouts. All of Bournemouth's normal standpipes, except for a few of the rather ancient "ball" type, were of the "lug" type until converted to "round-thread" under the 1938 Fire Brigades Act standardisation programme.

Concerned at the time spent by appliances and crews at chimney fires, hearth fires and small incidents, even minor gorse fires, and also requiring a vehicle for hydrant testing and inspections, Captain Wall proposed the purchase of a motor cycle and sidecar in October 1934. He changed his mind, however, the following month, and bought instead a Morris 8 horsepower chassis on which to build a van-type body. This was effectively constructed with adaptations by the Brigade's mechanics. Equipped with important essentials — standpipe, hose and various tools — it performed its purpose admirably, enabling no more than two men to handle situations and often only one man to remain at an incident and to supervise the clearing up and safety of the premises. This very practical innovation was sustained until the beginning of the Second World War.

A further secondary yet not unimportant acquisition resulted, in 1935, from Captain Wall's constant uneasiness concerning local petrol and oil storage. This took the form of a 60 gallon foam extinguisher, purchased from Foamite Firefoam Ltd., which comprised two 30 gallon cylinders mounted on a trailer complete with small armoured hose and cradle. Standing behind Central's pump, and ready for hitching, this apparatus was never used. It was replaced by a Pyrene Foam Branchpipe in April 1939.

Routine morning drills at Central commenced with a "pipe-opener", being a fast run up the escape which was kept permanently against the tower, and a descent of the inner cat-ladder. Brigade tradition emphasised speed as a direct product of the volunteers' era of competition, and Captain Wall (ever the volunteer) and Station Officer Alf Cook were equally insistent on it. Next each man carried out a "live rescue" without the comfort of a safety-line. Lastly, a one-man, two man or three-man pompier-ladder drill was carried out, with each man, on command and having secured his own belt-hook to the ladder ring, leaning well backwards with arms outstretched. These pompier-ladders — being forerunners of the more universal hook-ladders — originated in France in 1826, were taken up by United States brigades, demonstrated at the International Fire Exhibition at Earls Court in 1903, adopted by the London Fire Brigade, and bought by Bournemouth soon afterwards. They were 13 feet 5 inches in length, and consisted of a centre pole with climbing struts on each side, terminating in a 2 feet 2 inches barbed mild-steel hook and a 6 inch bill. Climbing was by way of hand-over-hand up the centre pole.

Drills were particularly highlighted each Thursday morning when, under the personal command of Captain Wall, the whole Brigade assembled in the Central Fire Station yard. The onlookers on the boundary walls were sure of a spectacle; it was Barnum without pause or make-up. A keen sense of humour was always a necessity in the life of a fireman, so these drills were looked upon as team entertainment. They were also a useful and indeed esssential exercise, and the noble Captain took a dim view of even a stifled chuckle. Practically every piece of equipment was brought to bear and smoke-bombs, being in fact Corporation drain-testers, were much in evidence. Various line rescues were suddenly called for, from sliding down singles from the top floor of the tower to leaping out on to twin lines in a type of abseil. Being the youngster, I was all too often the subject of binding to a scaling ladder and being craned down from the extended turntable ladders. Even the ambulance was alerted out of its garage in the yard, and Siebe Gorman's Novita Resuscitating Apparatus brought into use. Although a large green canvas jumping sheet was carried on the Turntable Ladders, it was used only infrequently and from the tower's first floor, as landing was rather hard and risky. Some of the old escapes were particularly heavy, and the effort and speed of their exercise was a pretty severe test of both muscle and lungs. One recalls the requirement of standing to attention at the end of a drill when nature would have preferred a more relaxed stance. A faint was often real. Tall Joe Thackwray once fell rigidly to the ground.

The 85 feet Turntable Ladders had to be climbed. In mid-air this was something of a challenge which at least two men openly refused. Although the lower extensions were rigid enough the top was as flexible as a short extension ladder. As it had no platform, standing upon it at full extension, particularly in a breeze, was an experience taken not too much for granted as one swayed anxiously. In case of mechanical breakdown, its elevation, extension and rotation could be operated by hand.

Apart from Volunteer Bob Dymott's fall in 1931, whilst abseiling from the top floor of the drill tower, only one serious accident occurred during the fairly risky drills at the Central Fire Station. This involved Fireman Bert Butt, an excellent chap who was a boot-repairer by trade. All Brigade footwear was meticulously cared for and his hand-stitching was such as was rarely seen elsewhere. He joined the Brigade in January 1931. Taking part in a three-man pompier-ladder drill with Ken Devereux and Tommy Upward, an ex-Royal Blue coach driver who also joined in 1931, he found himself in difficulty on the morning of 5 November 1931.

At 83 years of age he recalled: "I was number two and Ken Devereux was number three. We had all climbed up to the top of the tower. I got down to the first floor window and Ken had reached the ground. Tommy then took out the ladder from the top window and let it down to me, but unfortunately I lost the balance of it. I should have let it go and fall to the ground, but instead I tried to regain the balance. It all happened so suddenly: the top ladder fell, twisted my ladder, and the two ladders and I ended up on the ground."

He suffered a severe ankle fracture from which he never properly recovered. He woke up in hospital: "It was around seven o'clock in the evening when I was coming back into consciousness after an operation, and I could hear fireworks being let off. The nurse told me afterwards that I was shouting at the top of my voice 'Hoo-bloody-ray' as the fireworks went off." Upon his release from regular treatment in January 1932, the Lighting and Fire Brigade Committee agreed to discharge him with a Workman's Compensation Grant of £25, but the

Council ruled that this was too generous. So, limping somewhat, he resumed duties with the Brigade, mostly on ambulance work, until September 1936, when it was ruled that he was physically incapable and he was offered a position with the Lighting Department, as a lamplighter, at £2 7s 6d per week. In righteous indignation he refused, and for more than a year his legal adviser negotiated for a pension on his behalf. This was achieved in November 1937 when he was awarded the princely sum of 13s 9d per week, starting from 15 October 1936, and to be reviewed every twelve months.

The old chief: Captain H. Wall was the sixth and last volunteer chief of Bournemouth Fire Brigade, 1921-38.

Memorable fires

What can one record about fire calls and incidents in the 1930s? Generally speaking they seemed to arrive in spates, as no doubt they still do. Most were of a minor variety with a fair number of chimney and hearth fires. Those were the days of open fire grates, kitchen ranges, and various fossil fuels requiring the services of a host of busy chimney-sweeps. Stirrup pumps had not yet arrived, nor were the London antics of dispensing jets of water down chimney pots considered to be either clean or intelligent. Bournemouth's method was to remove the burning coals before jamming a wet sack into the chimney's lower orifice, thus suffocating the fire. A fireman would then be left to remove the sack, see that all was well and tidy up before impressing upon the occupant the urgent requirement of a reliable sweep. It proved very effective.

Fires of note included that which gutted Lulworth Castle on 29 August 1929. Although Bournemouth Brigade only stood by, it was a fair blaze, attended by Swanage, Dorchester, Weymouth and Poole Brigades under the command of Captain Colmer of Swanage, a keen and adroit fireman and no doubt equally proficient in his dental surgery. He often visited us.

At 5 am on a cold 21 January 1930, the boys at Canford School hurriedly evacuated their buildings and Poole Brigade, under Captain Matthews, Wimborne Brigade, and Bournemouth's seven-man Pokesdown crew under Captain Wall, made their way through thick fog. With the roof well alight, the Bournemouth lads ran out 1,000 feet of hose. Reg Wyeth's brass helmet saved him from serious injury when a beam fell and knocked him out.

During the summer of 1930, Station Officer Cook (nicknamed "The Admiral") instructed me to call him in the event of a fire call, so that he himself might take the call. This for no apparent reason. Soon afterwards, on 18 August, an excited voice on the telephone announced: "Picture House — fire", and the caller hardly waited for the arrival of Mr Cook who at no great pace waddled from the extremity of the yard.

Which picture house was it, out of the ten strewn around the Borough? A twitching, purple-faced Admiral was relieved when Pokesdown informed him on the direct line that the Savoy Cinema, Boscombe, was well alight. Only four weeks earlier, this old-established and now refurbished cinema had been known as "The Picture House, Boscombe": hence the confusion. It was 2.55 pm when smoke first billowed into the auditorium from a fire in the rewinding room. Mickey Mouse was on the screen as the small audience hastened their escape before the whole building became an inferno. The roof fell in and all was gutted. Dear old ex-Captain Robson (volunteer Captain from 1912 to 1921) from his nearby shop in Christchurch Road, was seen trying to assist in the operations.

On 20 August 1931 there was a fair blaze at Jenkins's Joinery Works in Muscliff Road, Winton, with damage valued at £2000. There was a thrill for hundreds of Old Christchurch Road shoppers on 12 May 1934 as five appliances attended a sizeable fire at the Williams and Hopkins store. 1934 was in fact the year of very considerable gorse and plantation fires, particularly on Lord Malmesbury's estate around Hurn, which involved working with Christchurch and Ringwood Brigades and many days of river pumping. Brownsea Island caught fire on 18 July and burned for seven days. It was reported that thousands of rats, which the somewhat eccentric owner, Mrs Florence Bonham-Christie, refused to destroy, swam to the mainland.

An interesting "job" was provided by the Bath Hotel at 3.25 am on 5 August 1936 in its King's Hall, which was a popular dance hall and thought to be a cut above the Pavilion as a tea-dance rendezvous. It was there that Deputy Chief Ken Devereux introduced me to the "art of smoke-eating"as, ignoring breathing apparatus, the two of us crawled snake-like the whole length of the hall and extinguished the burning stage and surroundings with a hose-reel jet. The smoke from the burning material was indeed extremely thick. The following day, the hotel's general manager telephoned to ask how the fire was extinguished as there was no sign of water, and he followed up with a letter of appreciation to the Council. This incident illustrated the faith in and the use of well-directed hose-reels, particularly in the early years of Bournemouth's professional brigade, which prevented much unnecessary water damage. Always at the ready, but kept in reserve, was the "big hose" and the London-control branches. Old Station Officer Cook always insisted, "You don't save property by flooding".

Emergency ambulance service

On 13 February 1930, the Lighting and Fire Brigade committee received a request from the Health Committee, following an approach by Superintendent Deacon of Bournemouth Police, to take over the running of the Street Ambulance Service. For many years the police, at their Madeira Road headquarters as well as their earlier Boscombe Station, had carried out this function as best they could. It was recalled that even prior to horse-drawn ambulances, the police used to push casualties for miles on structures known as "hand-ambulances". The first motor ambulance was delivered to them in 1924, but there was always a serious shortage of drivers so that the duty-driver was given a beat within the vicinity of Madeira Road. It was not uncommon to see a policeman running through the passageway of Motor Macs, opposite the Central Fire station, in order to hail his colleague pounding Holdenhurst Road.

On 10 April 1930, Captain Wall submitted his report, which whilst agreeing to the proposition, emphasised that the service would be for accidents only, two firemen, alternately amongst Central Fire station staff, would be on ambulance duty at all times, and he would not accept what he described as the "Black Maria" ambulance which was then in use. A modern vehicle had to be made available which, pending the construction of a permanent building, would be housed in a temporary garage to be erected in the fire station yard. In the event, a new Dennis ambulance, which cost £775, was delivered and the Brigade's "instant service" commenced at 12 noon on 29 October 1930 with Arthur Hatton at the wheel.

The Health Committee hedged on the question of paying the wages of two men, having had this vital service on the cheap for so long. It did eventually agree, on 16 March 1933, to pay for one man, and on 20 June 1935, the wages of a second man. By October 1937, in consideration of costs to the Brigade, the fairly considerable number of calls, especially during the summer months, and the increasing degree of upkeep, the whole of the service came under review by both committees, and the Lighting and Fire Brigade Committee agreed to take over the whole of the Borough Ambulance administration. This process, however, was checked in view of the other considerable burdens which were about to descend upon the Fire Brigade.

Whatever the doubts about running a combined service, in Bournemouth it operated excellently. Every man serving at Central took his round of duty and there was soon established a genuine keenness, in fact a new sense of dedication and an interest both in variety and meeting the unexpected. Night turn-outs were not exactly welcome, and there were strange encounters. For instance, I recall picking up a corpse at 3 am and conveying it to that rather ghastly little mortuary, lit by a small gas-jet, near the Central Railway Station. By a comradely agreement with the mortuary staff, we stripped the dead man of his clothes, covered him with a sheet and silently bade adieu to all the inmates of that solitary slab-furnished room. Calls ranged from faints to suicides, from slight falls to gory road crashes, and resuscitation on the beach. One could be more colourfully reminiscent; it was all a great experience and a thankful relief from the boredom of continuous duty.

First Aid classes, under the tutorship of Dr Heygate Vernon, were both serious and interesting. Commencing on 18 November 1930, all Brigade members were obliged to take three courses, with examinations at yearly intervals. The instruction was based on the St John Ambulance curriculum and certificates were presented on 14 April 1932 by Mr W. D'Angibau, Chairman of the Bournemouth Centre of St John Ambulance Association, and on 13 June 1934 by the Mayor of Bournemouth. Final medallions were presented on 19 March 1936 by Commander Turner, Chairman of the Health Committee. Dr Vernon, a splendid and much loved medico, was also chief gynaecologist at Boscombe Hospital, and he was concerned that in our travels, we should know precisely how to deliver a baby.

On 1 October 1934 a second ambulance (Morris, AEL 932) was put into service, and appropriately, a second two-man crew was made available. This was as well and particularly expedient when, during August-September 1936, there was a serious outbreak of typhoid in Bournemouth. By 18 September, 286 cases were receiving treatment and 19 deaths had been reported. The Local Health Authority was in some confusion, and was accused by Mr Leonard Lyle, our Member of Parliament, of "hushing things up". Not only were the Brigade's two ambulances heavily engaged in this emergency situation, and in conveying patients to Haddon Hall, on Haddon Hill, which was hurriedly prepared as a temporary hospital, but an old Sunbeam ambulance, which had been handed over to us by Boscombe Hospital in 1930 and used as a utility van, was also called into service.

Despite the extremely exhausting conditions which were to follow after 1937 for the Central lads, the Brigade carried out its ambulance duties until the fateful National Fire Service takeover on 18 August 1941, when the ambulances were handed over to the First Aid and Casualty Service of the Air Raid Precautions without ceremonial, much less any tribute to a great team of Fire Brigade professionals. Prior to that final event, a third ambulance with more modern facilities (an Austin costing £857) was delivered in September 1939 and the now well-worn Dennis was converted into a hose-carrier. Incidentally, the only accident involving an ambulance occurred on 26 December 1938 when, manned by George Cooper and Ivor Bolt, our "Blood Wagon", as it was irreverently called, encountered a milk lorry at the junction of Charminster Road and Richmond Park Road. There were no casualties.

MR. W. H. BARKER,
the new chief officer of the Bournemouth Fire Brigade.

The new chief: Bournemouth's first professional leader, Chief Fire Officer W.H. Barker, took over in April 1938.

23

The Brigade expands

The Brigade's growing manpower reflected the requirements of the Ambulance Service. Although the emphasis remained upon the importance and usefulness of employing firemen skilled in their own trade, preference inevitably had to be given to those who were also adroit heavy-goods drivers, and combined abilities were a bonus. Following Arthur Hatton, Peter Dorey, Bert Butt and Tommy Upward, at the end of 1930, we welcomed Reg Wescott, an inshore sailor and an expert on the repair of ropes and knot-making. His Braunton accent, from north Devon, had often to be translated. Norman Gilbert, who arrived in 1931, was a carpenter, and incidentally a sparring partner of the great boxer Freddy Mills. Mac McCabe, ex-coach driver and top class motor-cycle racer, stayed awhile but preferred his sport. Jack Whiting, another ex-coach driver for whom a special large helmet had to be made, was a grand chap but could not stand the duty, and Wally Churchill left for the same reason. Ivor Bolt joined in 1932, Len Bailey, a plumber, came in September 1933, Harry Andrews, a tyre specialist from Dunlops, joined in March 1935. Other arrivals were: Dickie Law, electrician, 1 January 1936; Hector Breaks, engineer and son of Chief Officer Tom Breaks of Sheffield, 1936; Arthur Linter, 1937. Basil Stocks joined whole-time on 9 April 1934, after serving eight years as a volunteer, and Stan Britt took over as Brigade Electrician when Alf Brooke resigned, becoming whole-time in January 1937 after serving for over twelve years as a volunteer.

Let us return to 1 October 1935, for it was on that day that Station Officer Alf Cook retired, quietly and unobtrusively as typified him. There were no speeches and no presentations — only an illuminated testimonial, sent later from the Council. Having no family of his own other than his very charming and modest wife, he no doubt felt conscious of the generation gap which separated him from the lads who in their turn saw him in his various shades of Victorian grouch. He forbade smoking anywhere on the station during working hours, although his own cigarette butt forever clung to his lower lip, especially in the office, where it was quickly stifled on the appearance of "Father" (Captain Wall). Nor was any intoxicating liquor, or any female visitor, allowed upon Central's hallowed ground. Any slight complaint brought the Admiral's sharp retort: "Yelverton Road, my son?"

Yelverton Road was then the home of the Labour Exchange

and the local dole queues were very long; the national unemployment figure for 1931 was 2,800,000. Joining the Brigade in 1900, he became a paid station fireman in April 1908 and a qualified driver of the first (Morris) motor engine in 1913. Promoted to the rank of Senior Fireman in 1921, and to that of Station Officer in April 1929, he was 59 when he retired to become Mine Host at the Red Lion Inn at Mortimer West End, where he died in 1950 at the age of 74.

Out of the 46 applicants, Ken Devereux, the Brigade Engineer, who had been acting as the Station Officer's deputy, was appointed Deputy Chief Officer at a salary of £250, rising by annual increments of £10 to £300, plus the usual emoluments, to take effect from 1 October 1935. Joe Thackwray who, as a fireman, had carried out inspections under the Petroleum (Consolidation) Act 1928 in October 1930 (receiving an additional 5s per week), was appointed to the rank of Station Officer and then took over the various additional inspections including The Pavilion, Theatre Royal and Hippodrome under the Theatres Act 1843, and all the cinemas under the Cinematograph Act 1909, as amended in 1930. At the Council meeting of 2 September 1930 the theatre licences were made dependent upon the managements agreeing to a direct telephone line with the Central Fire Station.

Notwithstanding Station Officer Cook's understandable sense of conservatism, his eagle eye was somewhat confounded when, as early as 1929, the younger men at Central began to conceive their own ideas about their conditions of service and expressed a desire to ally themselves to the growing struggle within the Service for a little more freedom and recognition. There was opposition to the threat of pay cuts, which echoed the concern in other large towns and cities. Somewhat surreptitiously, Connie Wyeth and the others met Jim Bradley, the first General Secretary of the Firemen's Trade Union, early in 1929. It was from that meeting that this great pioneer, already a sick man, returned to his London home and died. The Firemen's Trade Union became the Fire Brigades Union in 1930 and Percy Kingdom, its second General Secretary, also visited Bournemouth. In 1934, Connie Wyeth, Peter Dorey and Arthur Hatton invited me to join them in producing a "Bournemouth Fire Brigade Charter". Regrettably that historic document no longer exists and memory of detail is a little faded, but the main clause envisaged a three-shift system of duty which at that time almost boggled the imagination. We held a number of clandestine meetings in the unoccupied lower flat of No 14 Cotlands Road.

Numbers 4 to 14 Cotland Road had been purchased by the Council and converted into twelve flats for married firemen, by the industry of the Brigade's mechanics, in 1932.

To his credit, Captain Wall was well aware of his men's limits both of freedom and wage outlook. He brought up the latter subject at a Lighting and Fire Brigade Committee meeting on 11 October 1934, and following a sub-committee report, all pay other than that of the three sub-station firemen (Frampton, Williams and Baker) was increased by two shillings per week from 1 April 1935. These three veterans' gross wage of £3 16s per week was eventually increased by the Committee to that of the other married men now occupying the Cotland Road flats, at their meeting on 11 November 1937, which also proposed a new incremental scale which aimed at a maximum of £4 10s for firemen to take effect from 1 April 1938. This latter was promptly rescinded by the Finance Committee pending an eventual statement by the prospective professional Chief Officer Barker, who eventually submitted his recommendations on 18 June 1938, reaffirming a fireman's net wage of £4 10s per week, to which the Committee agreed, but which was again referred back by the Finance Committee and was never concluded.

The single men, who had been in receipt of an extra 10s per week as compensation for their uncomfortable living conditions, were accommodated in individual cubicles after the Central Fire Station alterations of 1937, and the watchful Council deducted that amount as rent as from 4 January 1938. Captain Wall was upset at this decision, and interviewed the men on 7 January following their Union meeting the previous day. Again, no action was taken pending the commencement of duty of a new Chief Officer, scheduled to arrive on 1 April 1938. As from 6 November 1934, additional leave was granted in the form of a half-day every alternate Sunday (mornings 7 a.m. to 1 p.m., followed by afternoons 1 p.m. to 11 p.m.). Later and in addition, a three-day weekend was accorded every six weeks from May 1936.

In spite of the conditions of service in the 1930s, involving restrictions which made continuity of courtship by the single men somewhat difficult, the comradeship and esprit-de-corps amongst everyone in the Brigade was of the highest order. Good humour prevailed, as did a genuine team spirit, both during the long hours on the station, and very much on the fire-ground. The Brigade's performance at fires did not rely particularly upon orders from officers, although old Station Officer Cook and Captain Wall were great and well-seasoned firefighters, and there were times when no officers were in attendance. One learned that the essential requirements for good and efficient firemanship were agility, ability, common sense and above all, a natural sense of liaison. Indeed, as a police officer was "an officer of the law", so a fireman was an officer of his profession. The Bournemouth Fire Brigade was a complete and reliable team. Social life and interests other than station work, which incidentally kept the mechanics busy enough apart from ensuring the fairly immaculate condition of both premises and appliances, were obviously confined. Motor-cycle tinkering and revving in the drill yard at Central allowed some of us to roar away helmetless at 7 am on our leave days. Joe Thackwray had a powerful Cotton, Arthur Hatton a Rudge Whitworth, Len Bailey a new 500 cc Hudson, Harry Andrews a BSA, and I an AJS, on which I passed my all-category driving test on 31 August 1936. Billiards rather than snooker occupied what was considered to be one of the finest tables in the town. Claude Faulkiner and his associates, notable local players, gave exhibitions on it, and periodic matches between the Brigade and the Police were keenly fought during enjoyable evenings. The phenomenon on those occasions was the traditional match between Captain Wall and Police Superintendent Deacon, who was so tall as to hardly need a cue-rest.

We held Christmas parties for children in Central's appliance room, which were followed by dancing to a three-piece band, and whist drives in aid of the NFBA's Widows' and Orphans' Fund. A recreation committee was formed on 19 January 1935, composed of Peter Dorey, Ivor Bolt, Alf Brook, Joe Thackwray and myself, and on 27 September 1935, we held our first annual Fire Brigade Ball at which 700 ticket holders (at 2s 6d a head) danced to the Pavilion's Sim Grossman and his Band. Again in aid of the NFBA Fund, it proved to be a major event in the town. Six feet high eye-catching posters surrounded the town centre, and Connie Wyeth scrounged such an enormous number of prizes from shopkeepers that Sim had difficulty in finding sufficient dance novelties.

This event, repeated until 1938, drew in performers from current stage shows. The Recreation Club's own finances were eventually supported by a grant of £6 10s per quarter, from May 1938, by a growingly magnanimous Council. The National Fire Brigades Association itself held its annual conference at the Town Hall, Bournemouth, on 25 September 1935 with 150 delegates representing about a thousand brigades.

Fire cover – new resources

Captain Wall's sense of realism, which was creating adequate fire protection for Bournemouth both in manpower and material, knew no bounds. As soon as it became his responsibility, he was conscious of an expanding area of fire risk. In 1929, for instance, the Council received over a thousand plans for new houses and shops. On 1 April 1931, Holdenhurst, Throop and Kinson added a further 4,627 acres to Bournemouth's territory, and Hengistbury Head brought 357 acres of gorse and woodland in 1932.

His aim was a much larger and more modern Central Fire Station and to close both Westhill Road and Winton stations. Although the avenues of consent led in the direction of the former, his emphatic and very detailed reports concerning centralisation met with strong reactions in the Council Chamber that reflected public fear and protest. Following the Lighting and Fire Brigade Committee's discussion of 16 May 1929, Mr F.P.Dolamore, the Borough Architect, himself a past volunteer member of the Brigade, was instructed to investigate the matter and report back. This he did on 12 September 1929. Unable to visualise a satisfactory rebuilding or alteration to the present Central Fire Station, he recommended the use of land on the site of the Lansdowne School grounds adjoining Madeira Road Police Station on which to build a new fire station which would work, as it were, alongside the Police. Major Cockburn, the Chief Constable, raised no objections. The Council set up a sub-committee composed of the Mayor (Alderman Cartwright), Alderman Robson, Alderman Thwaites, Councillor Tiller and Alderman F.S.Mate, the chairman of the Lighting and Fire Brigade Committee, which together with Captain Wall, sat on 14 November 1929 to consider the question of an extension to the existing building, whilst another sub-committee concentrated its efforts upon the Borough Architect's proposal. A combined report was considered on 16 January 1930, which favoured the extension of and alterations to the existing Central Fire Station.

The land required was occupied, at 30 Holdenhurst Road, by an old cottage. This was the home of the Smith family who, apart from living there, used its frontage as a fancy dress shop, and efforts proceeded to find them alternative accommodation. In order to produce ideas and plans which would meet all modern requirements, a deputation consisting of the Committee's Chairman, the Deputy Borough Architect and Captain Wall visited the main fire stations at Leicester, Aston (Birmingham), King's Norton, Mitchell and Butler's Brewery and West Bromwich on 10 July 1930.

An application to borrow the sum of £1,800 for purchasing the land required for the extension and a single-storey block at its rear for workshops and an ambulance garage was made to the Ministry of Health in October 1930. In the following month an estimate of £10,500 for the construction of the new buildings was agreed but the whole scheme seems to have been shelved for eleven months until, at its 10 September 1931 meeting, the Committee considered thirteen tenders from contractors which were referred to the Economy Committee. This Committee in turn recommended acceptance of a tender by Messrs. Hawkins of £11,222 plus £680 in respect of additional heating. There was, however, a little heat in the Council Chamber on 3 November 1931, when by a single vote it was agreed to postpone further action.

On 14 July 1932, at a time when the Cotlands Road property appeared to be a matter of piecemeal purchase, Captain Wall resumed an urgent appeal for the workshops and garage to be built. This the Council agreed to, and a tender by C.A.Barnes (£1,300) was accepted by the Committee on 25 November 1932, when it was also agreed to instruct the National Benzole Company to install a petrol pump in Central's yard at a cost of £50.

Meanwhile, in addition to our firemen/mechanics' work on the Cotlands Road property, they had the very unpleasant and itching job of demolishing the Holdenhurst Road cottage. It was unpleasant not only on account of the dirt and minute livestock, which was objectionable enough, but also because of a crowd of angry unemployed men, gathered in Holdenhurst Road and shouting abuse. A letter had been received by the Lighting and Fire Brigade Committee on 13 October 1932 from the Secretary of the Building Trades Operatives objecting to the use of firemen for the work which they felt their members were entitled to do. A special trade union meeting, held at Labour Hall, stated that "it was their business to consider whether a public body had the right to trample roughshod over the carefully built-up building industry". The Town Clerk replied with an explanation of the Council's policy governing the employment of Bournemouth firemen.

The Central Fire Station saga continued into 1935 until eventually, following a recommendation by a sub-committee set up on 14 November 1935, approval for a loan was given by the Ministry of Health and tenders were invited. Six were received and that of F.C.White (Boscombe) Ltd.(£10,195) was accepted on 27 July 1936. Coincidentally, Mr White was the son of Volunteer Fireman F.W.White, our hero who had been honoured for his rescue of two children at Pokesdown in 1898. Fifteen months later, on 28 October 1937, the great day arrived when the Mayor (Alderman Rebbeck) officially opened "The New Central Fire Station". Despite the huge crowd which gathered, comprising members of the Council, ex-volunteer firemen and visitors, the Brigade put on a drill display which was so realistic, that alternating between acting as commentator and fire-raiser, I managed to burn off the new paint on the tower window shutters with my own manufactured chemical flame. Long Service Medals were presented to Captain Wall (35½ years), Joe Frampton (24 years), Ted Williams (19 years), Bill Baker (13 years), Stan Britt (13 years), Peter Dorey (13 years), Arthur Hatton (12 years), Basil Stocks (11½ years), Joe Thackwray (10 years) and Reg Wyeth (10 years).

The old original side of the station now boasted a tiled appliance room floor; eight cubicles on the first floor for single men, plus an ablution room; on the second floor a Station Officer's flat in the front and a single-men's mess room and kitchen in the rear. The roof space now contained bathrooms, showers and a toilet. A single 47 feet brass cased steel pole connected all floors. This was reputed to be the longest pole in the British Fire Service. The old stables were now the Chief Officer's office, the Clerk's office and the Control Room, with an ablution room and toilets at the end of the block. The new side of the station, with the old workshop and toilets now removed, had the Chief Officer's flat on the first floor, the Deputy Chief's flat on the second floor, and the billiards room on the top floor.

The single-storey block, built in 1934, consisted of an ambulance garage, a store, a general workshop mainly used by the carpenters, a machine shop containing a lathe and hose repair equipment, and finally, at the top end of the drill yard as previously described, an engineer's workshop complete with pit and lifting gear. Aided by a Home Office grant, a further storey was built for the use of the Auxiliary Fire Service above the garage, store and general workshop in October 1938 at a cost of £1,230, which consisted of store rooms and a lecture room.

As in the case of the Westbourne district, protests had been flowing in concerning the possible closure of Winton Fire Station. These came particularly from residents in the outlying areas of Kinson, Throop, Ensbury Park and Wallisdown. Captain Wall, pressured also by conceivable Air Raid Precaution requirements, was having to reconsider his proposals. A new factor too was personified in Councillor H.A.Benwell, previously a councillor of the Kinson Ward which had joined Bournemouth in 1931, who was, by 12 November 1936, Chairman of the Lighting and Fire Brigade Committee. He succeeded Edwardian Alderman Mate, in the chair for so many years, who died on 3 February 1938. Captain Wall put in yet another request on 15 July 1937 for a new 2-bay station in north Bournemouth and asked for a suitable site to be found.

A special sub-committee was appointed on 16 December 1937 which duly recommended the purchase of land at the junction of Oswald Road and Redhill Park Drive (now Redhill Avenue). It was subject to confirmation by the prospective professional Chief Fire Officer after April 1938. Chief Officer Barker gave his approval on 12 May 1938, and the Ministry of Health was promptly asked for a loan of £1,920 in respect of the land.

The plans, prepared over the following few months and completed in April 1939, included an underground air raid shelter and certain Auxiliary Fire Service facilities and a proportion of the total cost, estimated at £20,000, was agreed as rating for grant by the Home Office on 28 July 1939. But Adolph Hitler was already on the march and that new fire station had to wait nearly 21 years. On 14 December 1939, the Council's Allotment Committee was given permission to use the land for wartime agricultural purposes.

Westhill Road Fire Station, so much the subject of shuttlecock debate, was threatened once again at the Council meeting of 7 December 1937, when a motion to close and to sell it was moved in line with previous policy and confirming an undertaking to centralise given to the Ministry of Health. Councillor Thomson, championing the objectors, moved the reference back, which was carried. It was decided to leave this matter again to the discretion of the new professional Chief Officer, who in fact, agreed on 14 April 1938 to allow the station to be used as an Air Raid Precaution store, and for the flat above to be let. But minds were changed, and on 23 August 1938, the ARP Committee was given one month's notice to quit, and on 15 June 1939, the tenant of the flat was similarly advised. So, with Fireman Reg Wescott in charge and with a team of auxiliary firemen, Westhill Road Station was once again on the run.

In his five-year capital expenditure programme, presented on

1 September 1938, Chief Officer Barker put forward an urgent proposal for enlarging Pokesdown Fire Station which involved an approximate cost of £5,000. On 20 April 1939, the Borough Architect submitted a plan for adding two further storeys for the purpose of accommodating a total of four married men and two single men. In addition, the Finance Committee approved the sum of £3,800 for the purchase of land at the rear of the station on 13 July 1939. But the Führer interfered with this project also.

The administration of the Brigade was much preoccupied by the projection of ideas and plans during the latter period of the 1930s, mostly initiated by Volunteer Captain Wall, who at the same time realised the unwisdom of being too precipitate, in view of his impending retirement and the onset of a new authority and the dawn of a new era. He had done so much to stimulate the interest of the Council into an understanding of the requirements of a professional fire brigade, and let it be said, the ebullience of Chairman Benwell was particularly opportune.

In 1936, Captain Wall was concerned with the obstruction to fire appliances and ambulances in the town centre by increasing traffic, particularly during the holiday season. The last Bournemouth tram ran on 10 April of that year, and positioning of the more numerous trolley-buses, with their freer use of road-width, was a little less predictable. He got authority in November 1936 to have loudspeakers erected on lamp standards at the Lansdowne — where two traffic policemen were on duty as there was no roundabout at that time — and the Square. There was a warning bell at the Bournemouth Pier Approach. By July 1937, a very satisfactory system was in operation, devised and constructed by Stan Britt, the Brigade's electrician. It was now possible to inform the traffic police at these points of the approach and route of all appliances leaving the Central Fire Station. It was to the astonishment of the public when an inter-station announcement or remark, intended for the lads, resulted from a forgotten change-over switch.

In July 1936 Captain Wall's five-year scheme for new equipment included a 2-ton Utility Van chassis, a new 100 feet Turntable Ladder and a new Escape-carrying Tender. In the event, a new limousine-type Pump Escape was ordered from Leyland (£1,895) in June 1937. This type of safer and more compact appliance body was a comparatively new feature within the Service. Various experiments were advanced in other Brigades, and Captain Wall had seen for himself, as did the writer on an independent visit, the New World type at Chief Officer Charlie Tozer's Birmingham headquarters. It merely had enclosed sides. Ken Devereux spent much time working in co-operation with Leyland's staff on Bournemouth's specific requirement. In April 1938, Chief Officer Barker inspected Poole Brigade's new 50 feet Bailey sliding-carriage escape and arranged with Leyland for a similar escape (£400) to be fitted. The appliance was finally delivered on 23 September 1938 and placed on the run five days later.

On 14 July 1938, tenders were received for the supply of a new 100 feet steel Turntable Ladder to incorporate a 500 gallons per minute pump. The Magirus tender, being cheaper but of German manufacture, was turned down in favour of the one by Merryweathers (£4,013), who agreed to take the old wooden 85 feet machine in part-exchange (credit £100). Their new Turntable Ladder was delivered in June 1939. The age and condition of some of the appliances was now the subject of obvious concern, and personal contact with the Home Office gave Chief Officer Barker a degree of support which he required in bringing about their gradual disposal.

In August 1938, a letter from the Home Office was received by the Lighting and Fire Brigade Committee which sharpened its own interest, with Air Raid Precautions much in mind, and in the following month, the 1914 Escape Tender (EL 2343) was sold to Christchurch Council for £20. On 20 April 1939, a second dual-purpose appliance (6-cylinder, dual-ignition, 80bhp, 700 gallons per minute (gmp) was ordered from Leyland (£1,680) and was delivered in December of that year.

It was quite evident that Captain Harry Wall wished the opening of the rebuilt Central Fire Station to be his swan song. But neither time nor circumstance could yet release this remarkable Volunteer Chief. All other signs of the Volunteer Brigade had now been faded out. The old insurance company links and contributions had been dispensed with in November 1934. Modernisation of communications meant more public telephone kiosks and police boxes; and both bodies were encouraged to make themselves available for fire calls from the public. Systematic dismantling of street fire alarm posts took place in 1937, reducing them from 54 to 35, which gave a shorter bicycle ride for the firemen's weekly Thursday morning tests.

Another more visual and striking change took place in 1936, after one of Captain Wall's friendly visits to Chief Officer Tozer of Birmingham. Impressed, and with the suggestion we might copy, the undress uniform of the Bournemouth firemen became enhanced by a grenade which replaced the NFBA enblem. The new brass-edged peak cap boasted a brass grenade badge fronted by a silver Bournemouth coat-of-arms. On parade, we looked like a Brigade of Guards and the public stared with some renewed interest. Even the new night watchroom operator, First World War disabled veteran T.H.Johnston (appointed 26 November 1937, wage £2 10s per week) felt a certain rediscovered pride.

The annual Church Parade, held in November at the request of each newly-appointed mayor, became traditional over many years. The Fire Brigade, marching from Holdenhurst Road with shining brass helmets and white cotton gloves, always gave sparkle to those occasions, if not a little refurbished sanctity to the wearers. Another tradition was the Mayor's refreshment interlude at the Town Hall after the march back, invariably from St Peter's Church. The firemen were the only ones, other than members of the Council and officials, to be invited to partake of His Worship's hospitality. It was quite lavish, with stimulants and large cigars provided by the Borough's Establishment, and we marched back to the Fire Station in high spirits. This custom continued with the professional Brigade until 1938, which was the last occasion the brass helmets were worn.

Of historic note was the big parade of the 1930s. It marked the occasion of King George V's Silver Jubilee on 6 May 1935, when members of uniformed bodies of every kind, from a "modern major-general" to a scout cub, marched to Meyrick Park with flags waving and martial music blaring. One remembers Captain Wall's seeming discomfort on the parade ground. There was the almost hilarious occasion when, after several about-turn orders given outside the Town Hall, we heard his apologetic voice saying, "I'm round here boys".

Fire Brigade: badge of Bournemouth Fire Brigade, 1936-41.

Central Fire Station, Holdenhurst Road: built 1901/02. This new extension was declared open by Mayor T.V. Rebbeck on 28 October 1937.

Central Fire Station: rear view after the 1937 rebuilding, showing the yard and drill tower.

Peacetime flames: Firemen Janku, Dorey, Law, Britt and Wyeth in action at Stewart Road, Charminster, in 1938.

The Looming Catastrophe

The years which followed the 1914-18 war were times of slow recovery and recuperation. The horrifying slaughter of that four-year period was not entirely lost on those of us who were mere babes at the time, yet we were later acquainted with a history of mankind and the consistent narrative of man's passive acceptance of war and his brainwashed submission to totally irresponsible and maniacal leaders. Once again, in our own time, we sought the indefinable "normal" and an almost mythical peace. In but a short twelve years, a nation, just across the North Sea, seeking for a Führer forthright and adventurous, actually voted into power one of the most demonic characters ever to find birth on our planet. Oh, for leadership! Oh, for the mask of strength! Oh, simplicitas! But although the present generation and generations to come will marvel at the somnabulent attitude of our nations's war-lords during a period when Hitler's intentions, as clearly defined in his book *Mein Kampf* as far back as 1923, might well have been halted, so preventing the catastrophe to come and the upheaval which so penalised the more normal and civilised growth of our country and of the British Fire Service, the Government at least was persuaded to recognise its responsibility for the protection of the public from that which was clearly indicated during the closing stages of the 1918 aerial assault.

The first bomb dropped on British territory by enemy aircraft had been a single high-explosive, which landed near Dover Castle on Christmas Eve 1914. Fears of "things to come" were confirmed for this island people when London suffered its first raid on 31 May 1915. One ton of high explosive bombs was dropped from a German Zeppelin. The use of incendiary bombs has been previously mentioned, and was given a great deal of attention, certainly by Fire Brigade organisations, but the main point of uneasiness and concern, yet more ominous, was a gas attack by any future enemy. The subject of Air Raid Precautions appeared repeatedly on governmental confidential agenda for several years after 1918, and eventually the Government's Air Raid Precautions sub-committee held its first meeting on 15 May 1924, chaired by Sir John Simon. This became a full committee in August 1925, and developed into the ARP (Organisation) Committee in 1929, when consideration was being given to types of public shelters and the issue of gas masks. The latter subject received some agreement in 1934, whereby certain types of mask would, if necessary, be issued to the public, and special

Service masks to the Police and Fire Service. At this stage the confidentiality which had been intended to prevent public alarm could no longer be maintained, and at last, Mr Stanley Baldwin, Lord President of the Council in the Conservative-dominated National Government headed by Labour Prime Minister Ramsay MacDonald, made the following announcement in the House of Commons on 19 July 1934:

'We feel with regard to the protection of the civilian population that our plans have been carried as far as is possible without wider publicity than has hitherto been deemed to be in the public interest. The new stage involves communications with local authorities, with public utility companies, and so forth, and with all those on whom responsibility for action would fall in the emergency contemplated, and before long, steps will be taken to communicate the necessary instructions to the general public. Let us never forget this. Since the day of the air, the old frontiers are gone. When you think of the defence of England, you no longer think of the chalk cliffs of Dover, you think of the Rhine. That is where our frontier lies.'

Indeed Hitler, who had already become the new German Chancellor in 1933, was sweeping internal opposition aside and repudiating the Versailles Treaty, and already building up his Luftwaffe so much that, by the spring of 1935, he was boasting, even to Winston Churchill, that his air power was equal to our own.

What became very apparent in the minds of the various heads of government concerning the type of assault and tactics of any future foe was that the population, towns, cities and industry of the whole country could be so vulnerable to air attack as to be rendered powerless and so defeated. In short, Air Raid Precautions, or Civil Defence as it was later termed, and in particular effective protection from fire, was of prime importance. Notwithstanding the proposals which had been made from so many sources and which were largely contained in the report of the Royal Commission back in 1923, no real effort had yet been made, in the early 1930s, to legislate even for compulsory fire cover, much less for an effective liaison of brigades and an appraisal of equipment. Now, following the disclosures of the Home Secretary, the cry for action became increasingly irresistible. On 13 March 1935, Labour MP Ben Gardner asked the

Home Secretary, Sir John Gilmore: "In connection with the preparations foreshadowed for National Defence and the danger of incendiary attack from the air, is any scheme being worked out for bringing all fire brigades up to any approved standard and interlinking them for joint action?"

The Home Secretary confirmed the Government's acquiescence and stated that an appropriate committee was to be appointed to study the problem. The outcome was the setting up of the Departmental Committee on Fire Brigade Services by the succeeding Home Secretary, Sir John Simon, on 5 August 1935. The Committee's reference was: "To review fire brigade services in England and Wales and to advise whether any steps are needed to improve organisation and co-operation for the purpose of meeting danger from fire".

Lord Riverdale chaired the Committee of four which began its work on 30 September 1935 and completed its report in July 1936. The Riverdale Report based itself mainly on the outcome of the Royal Commission in 1923, and the points of view of some forty witnesses. The sixty-seven recommendations included the consolidation of fire brigade legislation, the free availability of fire protection, adequate fire protection measures to be obligatory upon all local authorities, a national system of inspection by the Home Office and a direct contribution by the Government for fire protection development, the setting up of training schools and standardisation of equipment.

In fact from 1935 to 1938, the Government was being faced with two grave factors regarding the British Fire Service, which were intertwined. Priority had to be given to a commencement of Air Raid Precaution organisation on a national scale, which needed the practical response of the better-established fire brigades, before tackling the uniformity of the Fire Service itself. By 4 July 1935, memoranda were circulating from the Secretary of State to all local authorities, advising on the setting up of Air Raid Precaution Committees and their essential administration, which would bring to bear a sense of urgency and a comprehension of what was to follow. The Government's own department had itself begun activities on 15 April 1935. The aim was to complete all its plans by 31 March 1939.

It is not my intention to elaborate upon the extensive ARP activities of the Government, nor upon Bournemouth's efforts of 1936-37, but very few of us, at local fire brigade level, realised at the time the pace of events which preceded the Air Raid Precautions Act of 1937. In 1936, for instance, experiments and trials were being conducted at various centres with incendiary bombs and such an exercise was carried out at Southampton early in 1937. The early and consistent concern over the possibility of extensive gas attacks had produced over 21 million civilian gas masks by the end of 1937 and the Civil Anti-Gas School at Eastwood Park, Falfield, had been training officers since 15 April 1936. Our Deputy Chief, Ken Devereux, took a course there in February 1938. Locally, representatives from Bournemouth, Poole and Christchurch met, by way of introduction, in August 1935. They set up a joint ARP Committee in accordance with the requirements of a Home Office circular of 9 July 1935. The Mayor of Bournemouth was appointed Chairman.

The Committee's second meeting, called because of the visit of Commander Frankson from the Home Office – who complained of apathy – did not take place until 6 May 1936. It included Captain Wall and Captain Bryant of Christchurch. Discussion, it seems, was confined to the questions of first aid and anti-gas measures and a sub-committee met with reference to these matters eventually on 4 October 1936. An appointed ARP officer, in the person of Captain M. Bell, DSO, MC, brought some semblance of activity on 4 August 1937 when costs were apportioned – Bournemouth was to pay 70 percent, Poole 25 percent and Christchurch 5 percent. Alderman Sir Charles Cartwright took over as Controller and Councillor Harry Mears, acting as Deputy Controller, became Chairman in November 1939, following Alderman Little, after a further push by the Home Office. Although representatives from the Fire Brigade (Deputy Chief Ken Devereux) and from the Police were required to attend, fire protection arrangements were not discussed. The story of the Bournemouth Air Raid Precautions organisation up to the time that Councillor Harry Mears took over as Controller from Sir Charles Cartwright in 1941 is not a happy one.

A plan for action

The culmination of some two-and-a-half years of concentration, numerous meetings and conferences, preliminary planning and construction of an immense project produced the Air Raid Precautions Bill which was presented to Parliament on 4 November 1937. It received its second reading on 15 November 1937 and became an Act on 1 January 1938. The law now imposed on all local authorities the responsibility for "the protection of persons and property from injury or damage in the event of hostile attack from the air", and for the urgent drawing up of schemes. Larger authorities were obliged to consider the requirements of surrounding districts. If the country as a whole was not already convinced, certainly a united Parliament was giving the lead. As Secretary of State Sir Samuel Hoare proclaimed: "This is an enormous new problem. It is new technically, new administratively and above all, it is new psychologically to our people."

In fact, the Air Raid Precautions Act opened the doors for action, and it would, by Orders, be amended and extended according to developments. Its whole plan was to be completed by 1941. In what might be termed "general civil defence"(the term "Civil Defence" in due course replaced "ARP") it meant the compulsory organisation of air raid wardens, casualty services, rescue and demolition parties, gas detection and decontamination and the distribution of gas masks, the provision of shelters and all necessary recruitment and training. Trenches were actually dug in Bournemouth in 1938 at a cost of £2,925, but became waterlogged. It was also required that the public should be appraised of both need and urgency and informed of air raid warning procedures. These were revolutionary requirements for normal peace-time conservative councils and Bournemouth certainly went through its initial process of making haste with the brakes on. Loud was the criticism for a while. The Mayor, Sir Charles Cartwright, remained as Group Controller. Progress would have to wait for Harry Mears's outstanding vision and natural ebullience.

The Air Raid Precautions Act 1937 gave the British Fire Service the signal which was so urgently needed. It was a directive of considerable and comprehensive proportions, requiring local authority schemes to be based on advice which was circulated early in 1938 by the Home Office Fire Brigades Division. All of this concept of possible wartime requirement emanated from the office of Mr (later Sir) Arthur Dixon, Assistant Under-Secretary of State, whose work in this field had been pressured since October 1936 and who had issued certain recommended measures in February 1937. This document, sent to all local authorities, concerned itself with what appeared at the time to be an almost undreamed of conception of fire cover, to be produced by local schemes requiring the approval of the Home Office, which itself would provide on loan a vast quantity of pumps and equipment for use by auxiliary firemen at auxiliary fire stations.

In March 1938, the Air Raid Precautions (Fire Schemes) Regulations itemised requirements to be based on the yardsticks of street mileage and of high, medium and low fire risks. Each scheme required, under what was termed the Emergency Fire Brigade Organisation (EFBO), detailed plans for the recruitment and training of auxiliary firemen, aged 25 to 50, medically examined and uniformed; storage and maintenance of quantities of pumps and equipment; the securing of towing vehicles; and emergency water supplies. It also required a review of peace-time personnel and appliances. The Act indicated the size of the project nationally when it estimated that initially no less than 20,000 Auxiliary Fire Service pumps and 3,000 miles of hose would be required.

For me, at the time engaged quite fully with peace-time fire brigade administration, this great deluge of responsibility boggled the imagination. As for Captain Wall, only an extraordinary sense of dedication and resolve had enabled him to cope with the pressures of 1937. The opening of the extended Central Fire Station might well have been a fitting swan-song, and his resignation was in fact accepted by the Lighting and Fire Brigade Committee on 26 November 1937. He was, however, asked to continue in his voluntary office until the appointment of Bournemouth's first professional Chief Fire Officer, scheduled for 1 April 1938.

So it was that, on 31 March 1938, the Bournemouth Fire Brigade bade farewell to a very gallant, kindly and respected gentleman. Within the Service itself, his work and renown, particularly in the Southern District of the National Fire Brigades Association, had been manifest for many years, and in April 1936, he was awarded the Association's Services Rendered decoration, one of its highest honours. His "boys", with their wives and friends, honoured him as their Chief for the last time at a dinner held in Central's appliance room on 23 March 1938, and presented him with an electric chiming clock. It was an intimate and memorable occasion for everyone. Even the most recently-appointed were conscious of its significance. Few indeed who listened to his reminiscent cogitation could take in the immensity of his service and fewer still could know of his considerable and responsible role as Head of the Brigade, having been so promoted from the rank of Third Officer in October 1921. Little did he realise when he joined the Brigade in January 1902, being the last to be enrolled under Captain Worth, that his would be the task of introducing and creating Bournemouth's professional Brigade under conditions almost completely foreign to those of his youth.

He told of the time when he was called to a fire by telegram, the message being handed in at Bournemouth, relayed to Boscombe and delivered by foot-messenger to his home nearly a mile away. Later, when telephones were more generally available, the fire station would convey a message to a grocer's shop, the grocer telling the man next door, who in turn would deliver somewhat incoherent information. He recalled his wife insisting upon his wearing his helmet at what he understood to be a "small job". It saved his life when guttering fell from the roof. Of his teetotal superiors, he told of an occasion when, with some temerity, he suggested that the men be allowed beer at their annual dinner: "It was like a bombshell when I put the suggestion forward. I was told such a thing was unheard of and there would be a clamour about the firemen going home drunk. However, the beer appeared on the tables and no one went home tipsy."

Sad it was to witness not only the retirement of the last Volunteer, but the end of a long and wonderful era of Bournemouth's history in which this man's dedication, devoted service and philanthropy shone: the exemplar of that which would never be witnessed again in the light of new conditions and philosophy. Those of us who worked, not so much under him as with him, were privileged indeed. The Bournemouth Council, for its part, presented to him in February 1938 an Illuminated Address and subscribed a "suitable honorarium". He died on 15 May 1950.

On 11 February 1938, the Lighting and Fire Brigade Committee, having received 83 applications for the post of Chief Fire Officer, interviewed W.H. Barker of Dagenham, M. Coles of Hornsey, K.A. Devereux of Bournemouth, A.H. Finney of Wolverhampton, J.Y. Kirkup of Bristol, R.H. Owen of Liverpool and T.E. Smith of Halifax. Thirty-nine-years-old William Howard Barker was appointed as Bournemouth's first professional Chief Fire Officer to commence duties on 1 April 1938. A Birmingham man, he came from a family of fire-fighters, his father having been an officer in the Birmingham Fire Brigade for 28 years. He had served an apprenticeship as an engineer at the Lanchester Motor Company before joining the Royal Navy Air Service in the First World War during which, as a petty officer mechanic, he was stationed in France, Salonika, Italy and the Aegean Sea. In 1923, he joined the London Fire Brigade and served for eight years in the busy Redcross Street Fire Station. He was the first man in the Brigade to sit for and pass the examination of the Institution of Fire Engineers of which he was currently a full member and a member of its Executive Council. Having been appointed Deputy Chief of Finchley Brigade in 1930, he obtained the chief officership of Dagenham three years later. His Bournemouth salary was £450 per annum, rising to £500, plus free quarters, heating and lighting. With no staff car then available, the driving of his own Austin Ten entitled him to a £50 yearly allowance.

He arrived in his office on 7 April 1938 and Deputy Chief Ken Devereux, Station Officer Joe Thackwray and I were summoned into The Presence. To speak of his immediate overpowering sense of command as shattering is almost an understatement. Without trace of formality, here was a supremo who wasted not a moment in affirming his authority, and seemed bristling with impatience to put his stamp upon everything and everybody.

Admittedly, although we were a pretty alert team at the Central Fire Station, general operational vigilance had not caught up with London Fire Brigade-type routine, not that Chief Officer Barker's first day's orders for "standard testing" brought much beyond amusement from the men as the first item to yield was the escape which had been stationed in the drill yard for years and on which we had drilled continuously. "Crack!" went the rounds as Harry Andrews jumped them in a way guaranteed to produce no other effect, and the strings (sides) split with little protest. The other brigade escapes proved the better for repair and the last of the pompier ladders was replaced by the modern type of hook ladder. Meanwhile, back in the office, the orders grew for new equipment, such as rescue lines and vapour-proof lamps. The pressure was on.

Beyond any sense of humour — always, let it be said, a major asset in the Fire Brigade — came a striking realisation by all concerned that a vital new chapter had begun. Like it or not, any semblance of inertia could no longer exist and both individually and collectively, life in the Bournemouth Fire Brigade, from that April morning, was never to be the same again. No one was going to take Chief Officer Barker to his heart but there was little hesitation in realising something of that with which he was faced. Captain Wall had endeavoured to pursue changing events as best he could, but a mounting residue had to be passed to his professional successor. From a peace-time (a new term) brigade point of view, Bournemouth was second to none in fire-fighting ability, but in Barker's London concept, we were "provincial". The Air Raid Precautions Act with all its ramifications had received no practical introduction and the doors of this vast project were already being opened wide. Fire Prevention, despite its limitations at that time, had yet to serve its rightful place of importance and routine.

At his first Lighting and Fire Brigade Committee meeting on 12 May 1938, Chief Officer Barker was formally appointed as Inspector under Section 60 of the Public Health Act 1936, and authorised to inspect building plans deposited with the Council. Station Officer Thackwray was authorised to continue his inspections of cinemas in line with the Celluloid and Cinematograph Film Act 1922 and the 1930 Amendment of the Cinematograph Act 1909. The other legislation with which the Local Authority was involved included the Factories Act 1937 and the Petroleum (Consolidation) Act 1928. The question of conditions of service, previously raised by Captain Wall, also awaited consideration. The subject of leave was unlikely to be progressively affected in view of what was about to be expected of all Brigade members, although the writer's "office hours" − with constant, extensive and unpaid overtime, were speedily introduced.

Captain Wall's endeavours on the pay structure were quickly taken up and the following proposals by Chief Officer Barker were unanimously agreed by the Lighting and Fire Brigade Committee on 16 June 1938:

Scale of net wages to be adopted as from 1st October 1938.

Station Officer . . . £4 10s per week, rising annually by
                     increments of 2s 6d per week to
                     a maximum of £5 10s per week.

Fireman . . . £3 2s per week, rising by four annual
             increments of 2s 6d per week to
             £3 12s per week, then by annual
             increments of 2s per week to a
             maximum of £4 10s per week.

Engineer . . . As fireman, with the addition of 5s
              per week Special Duty Pay.

The wages of the present staff to be increased by the addition of one increment for every three completed years of past service.

The Council, however, decided to refer this resolution back to the Finance Committee, which recommended "that the proposed commencing wage as from 1st October be approved, but that the increments operate for four years only, and that the increments to be awarded for past service be one increment for every six completed years of past service instead of one increment for every three years' service." And so it was!

Uniform was soon to be varied by the inclusion of heavy duty jerseys and waterproof leggings but the new contract was passed from Huggins of Bristol to Rego of London, and Mr Litt, who was acquainted with Chief Officer Barker, became a regular visitor. It was a cheaper quotation, but regrettably, a much inferior product. Considerable orders for nearly all the Auxiliary Fire Service uniforms were later to please the portly Mr Litt.

1938 must be the turning point in any Fire Brigade history, reflecting the increasing pressure which had grown over the years out of the Middlebrook Report and the Royal Commission, the constant influence of the Professional Fire Brigades Association and the National Fire Brigades Association, and the threat of war had been telling those responsible for the fire protection of our island, quite clearly, to put their peace-time house in order. It had taken a long time indeed for the message to sink in, for the Government to produce the logical requirements and for quite a number of local authorities to realise that penny-pinching on the "Cinderella Service" was a lost cause.

The transition inside some of the more imaginative brigades started in the mid-1930s. London's new Albert Embankment headquarters was opened by the King in July 1937, and the opening of Birmingham's huge new headquarters had preceded even that event by a year. Yet further back in time to 1935, a co-ordination scheme of fire protection was being organised in North Derbyshire. As we have observed, Bournemouth could take some pride in being reasonably well alerted, for as the newly-extended Central Fire Station had been completed in 1937, so new appliances were on the way, and the Brigade was now wholly professionalised.

The Riverdale Report had to be implemented and now the absence of proper legislation governing the peace-time service hardly fitted the urgent requirements of the Air Raid Precautions Act 1937. Sir Samuel Hoare, a Home Secretary with some experience of the Fire Service, duly called together representatives of his office and the local authority associations, and with the minimum of delay, the Fire Brigades Bill received a smooth second reading on 10 May 1938. In fact, the Bill shook not only the House of Commons but much of the country when it was realised that heretofore no compulsion had ever existed where fire protection was concerned. The Fire Brigades Act 1938 received the Royal Assent on 28 July 1938. Its provisions included:

(i) The designation of county boroughs and county districts as "fire authorities" (1,440 in England and Wales and 228 in Scotland), which must provide all facilities for "the extinction of fires and the protection of life and property in case of fire" free of charge (appliances, accommodation, communication systems, including fire alarms, water supplies, etc.). Fire Brigade duties were described.

(ii) Prescribed standards of efficiency, uniformity of equipment and a Home Office Inspectorate.

(iii) Satisfactory co-ordination arrangements for mutual help with surrounding authorities, with arrangements for payment.

(iv) Powers of entry by fire officers.

(v) The setting up of a Central Fire Brigades Advisory Council.

(vi) The establishment of training centres.

(vii) The extension of the Fire Brigades Pensions Act 1925 to include temporary firemen.

(viii) Reorganisational measures in police fire brigades.

(ix) The right to use AFS equipment at "peace-time" fires.

The particularly significant part of the Act reflected itself upon the importance of out-district relationships, which became extended by virtue of the 1937 Act with regard to "key-calling" brigades. Wimborne and Cranborne Rural District Council made enquiries of our Brigade in November 1938, but it was not until April 1939 that fire chiefs in the Hampshire areas conferred at Southampton in order to discuss the preparation of schemes as required by the Defence Regulations Emergency Powers Act 1939, Statutory Rules and Orders. The whole country was now divided into regions.

Our Region, No 6, comprised certain parts of the outskirts of London (later included in the London region), Buckinghamshire, Berkshire, Oxfordshire, Hampshire, part of Dorsetshire (as it was then known) and the Isle of Wight, and was divided into fourteen districts.

No 4, Bournemouth, district comprised the County Borough of Bournemouth, the Borough of Christchurch, the Borough of Lymington, the Borough of Poole and Dorset, the Rural District of Ringwood and Fordingbridge, the Urban District of Wimborne Minster and the Rural District of Wimborne and Cranborne. The whole district was under one unified control, with Bournemouth's Chief Officer Barker acting as District Officer.

It might well be considered that Chief Officer "Bill" Barker had taken over his Bournemouth responsibilities at a most appropriate time. He was able, on his own initiative, to construct and virtually to dictate the conditions which he required, and both planning and organisation were most certainly his particular forte. Backing him to the limit in all his adventures was the Chairman of the Lighting and Fire Brigade Committee, Councillor Harold Benwell, himself a particularly enterprising and ambitious "human dynamo". These two gentlemen had much in common and were complementary to each other.

"Bene" (or "Coco", as the Brigade lads nicknamed him) had also served in the First World War, when as a second lieutenant, he was awarded the Military Cross before being promoted to the rank of captain. Employed as an inspector by the Legal and General Insurance Company, and later by the Royal Insurance Company, whose business policies richly abounded the fire service, he was a member of the Bournemouth Round Table and, as was Chief Officer Barker, a Freemason. A JP, Councillor Benwell was later to become Bournemouth's youngest alderman, at the age of 44, in March 1941. On that occasion, by virtue of a round robin request sent out to all personnel on 13 March 1941 by Chief Officer Barker — an exercise strongly criticised in the Council Chamber — he was presented with his scarlet robes and tricorn hat by members of the Auxiliary Fire Service. He was eventually to become Mayor of Bournemouth on two occasions (1952 and 1964) and was made a Freeman of the County Borough on 25 July 1967. The first to join the Bournemouth Auxiliary Fire Service, part time, in 1938, he was appointed its Commandant in September 1939. He remained Chairman of the Committee until 1969, excepting his two periods as Mayor.

In the office, the Chief Officer's almost hourly decisions coupled with Councillor Benwell's constant supervenient requests, in addition to routine administration, were at times almost impossible to handle, and for many months entailed working into the early hours of the morning when peace and quiet reigned. By the middle of the summer of 1938, with the Emergency Fire Brigade Organisation duly launched and forging ahead, my own intense activity was somewhat relieved by the appointment of an AFS Clerk, and Mr Prothero commenced his duties on 23 June. Quiet, unassuming and hard-working, he found the Chief's demands and lack of patience impossible to cope with, and by November he voiced his dissent most audibly before packing his bags.

The appointment of Mr Ernest Woodrow, from 50 applicants, followed in January 1939, and fortunately for all concerned, being a middle-aged ex-civil servant of considerable experience and capacity, he was made of much sterner stuff. His sense of diplomacy was a match for the Chief who learned so to value him that he appointed him AFS Organising Officer in September 1939 with a pay rise of 10s a week. But for this he was obliged to live at the Central Fire Station and away from his family, and to be virtually available at all times — as was the writer who also received a five shillings per week rise. By this time, two shorthand-typists were also employed, at £1 15s per week each, and the ablution room, next to the Control Room, had been converted into an office. "Woody" and I became firm friends.

From April 1938, planning the Auxiliary Fire Service and the physical application of that planning were matters of immediate pursuit. We were faced with the enrolment of large numbers of auxiliary firemen, their training and their protective clothing, firewomen for control room training, men and women car owner-drivers for general transport and young messengers and despatch riders, coincident with the ordering of many trailer-pumps and their requirement of hose and equipment, plus the procurement of suitable towing vehicles. The plan rested upon "zoning" the County Borough and the acquisition of suitable auxiliary fire stations which could house both crews and appliances and act as centres of communication; and which would be focal points for patrol systems, the latter being part of the Home Office's early recommendations. Later, in the light of actual air-raid experience, this proved to be impracticable. All details of the Emergency Fire Brigade Organisation scheme had to receive the approval of the Home Office, which, in line with the 1947 Act, was to pay 75 percent of the cost of certain aspects. The endorsement of the Bournemouth Council was also required.

By the end of May 1938, parts one and two of the EFBO scheme had been passed by the Council. After an extensive survey, eleven provisional zone stations were agreed. These were to be at: (1) the Corporation East Yard in Holdenhurst Road; (2) the Corporation Depot in Palmerston Road; (3) the Corporation Depot in Morley Road; (4) the Corporation Depot in Norwich Road: (5) the Corporation Depot in Maxwell Road;

(6) Brewster's Garage, Belle Vue Road; (7) King's Garage, Stewart Road; (8) Sparrow's Garage. Kinson; (9) The Corporation Depot in Meyrick Park; (10) Strouden Park Hotel, Castle Lane; and (11) Rodd's Garage, Howeth Road. There had to be some serious re-consideration, for some of these premises were very unsuitable.

Within a matter of weeks, changes were made and eventually the final zoned stations were as follows: (1) Central Fire Station, Holdenhurst Road; (2) San Remo Towers, Sea Road; (3) Pokesdown Fire Station; (4) Westhill Road Fire Station; (5) Corporation Depot, Maxwell Road; (6) Akhurst Garage, Southbourne Grove; (7) disused church in Nortoft Road; (8) Pelhams, Kinson; (9) Corporation Depot in Meyrick Park; (10) Strouden Park Hotel, Castle Lane; (11) Lee Motors, Moordown.

Again as a preliminary, we estimated a requirement of 87 patrol units, each with crews of six to eight men, 80 light trailer pumps (120-150 gallons per minute at 80 lbs pressure), 11 medium trailer pumps (250-350 gpm at 100 lbs) and seven heavy pumps (700-900 gpm), with 57,000 feet of 2½ inch hose and 2,500 feet of 3½ inch hose, 100 towing vehicles, storage facilities and a number of specified water supplies. We considered that we needed 647 auxiliary firemen — 70 names had already been submitted by May 1938 — 100 messengers and 50 control room personnel.

Nationally, the Committee of National Defence, which examined the 1937 Act, considered a plan which it intended to complete by 1941. Events were already moving early in 1938, and by April, some 30,000 auxiliaries had been recruited. By June 1939, 900 local authority schemes had been accepted, involving 120,000 auxiliary firemen, and 18,000 control room attendants. 4,350 emergency appliances had been delivered, together with 470 miles of hose. Hose delivery, incidentally, became a problem because of a shortage of flax, and orders given to firms in France were also limited because of their own requirements. By the spring of 1939, we were receiving cotton-jacketed rubber hose from the United States, and Britain eventually received 3,400 miles. This hose was very durable but heavy. Hose couplings were 2½ inch, and all Bournemouth's peace-time 2¾ inch couplings had to be changed at a cost of £250. A similar modification involved the Brigade's standpipe heads at a further cost of £50.

OVERLEAF – Zone control: map of Bournemouth's eleven zone Emergency Fire Brigade Organisation scheme (with existing stations depicted by 'X' and the additional ones with an 'O'), presided over by Chief Fire Officer W.H. Barker (seated) and Station Officer Joe Thackwray.

The drive for recruits

For many weeks, during the summer of 1938, Chief Officer Barker and I were out in the town addressing groups, and in particular, the staffs of local businesses, in the cause of Auxiliary Fire Service recruitment, and arising therefrom, it was an extraordinary experience to have scores of men and young ladies — I wondered what old Station Officer Cook would have said — milling around in the evenings and being entirely dependent upon the control and organisational abilities of a handful of us at the Central Fire Station. At a minimum age of 25, each prospective auxiliary fireman was required to pass a medical examination and a proficiency examination after undergoing sixty hours of training, after which he would receive a bonus of £3 from a grateful Government. An insurance policy was agreed with the Northern Insurance Company which was based on a Home Office "schedule for injuries during training". Recruits also had to be approved by the Ministry of Labour. By June 1938, 303 application forms had been signed, and the following month, 500 posters decorated the County Borough. As an essential prelude to training, 100 pairs of rubber boots (at 7s a pair) and 100 overalls (at 7s 5d) were hurriedly purchased. In August, tenders were invited for the supply of 300 complete uniforms (£1,080), to include tunics, trousers, caps, belts and axes and leggings, plus 200 more pairs of boots, and overalls and blue armlets for messengers.

It might be well noted that Chief Officer Barker's somewhat personal relationship with the occupants of the Fire Brigades Division of the Home Office, to which he paid a particularly important visit in June 1938, greatly helped to shape our EFBO scheme, which was approved and commended in the August. Amendments of estimates, both of personnel and equipment, were inevitable as the picture, both nationally and locally, grew. In June 1938, the Chief's pump requirement had leapt to 303, which proved to be a highly exaggerated figure, but offers of 45 lorries (on loan) to be used as towing vehicles had already been received. In August, the first two Beresford Stork light trailer pumps arrived, and a further assortment consisting of one large pump, four medium pumps and a further 28 light pumps were on the way. Meanwhile, covering my office wall, there now appeared a huge map of the County Borough upon which was delineated the eleven zones and which was completed with a provisional mobilising board.

September 1938 brought crisis. Hitler had secured Austria in

March 1938, and as the months went by, the German threat was becoming more and more understood. In fact, war seemed to be inevitable until Prime Minister Chamberlain flew to Munich and returned with a "Peace in our time" message from the Führer and a pact designed to prevent his annexation of Czechoslovakia. We doubted not the charade. Enjoying a few days' break in the West Country, I received my Chief Officer's telegram: "Return at once", and found a queue of aspiring auxiliary firemen which reached nearly to the Lansdowne from the Central Fire Station. It was an extraordinary experience, signing on men whose faces were often familiar. Professional men, clerks, shop assistants, builders, mechanics, salesmen, musicians and even gigolos. With perhaps a touch of cynicism, one asked oneself why certain of them were wishing to join the local Fire Service as a war-time preference. Enlightenment was awaited.

What of the real Bournemouth Fire Brigade? Looking back, it seems to be almost a mystery as to how peace-time requirements were contained. Our three stations were on the run. Westhill Road station later resumed its role as a fire station in June 1939, manned by Staff Fireman Reg Westcott, aided by auxiliary firemen. Fires were given their usual speedy attendance, as were the usual number of emergency ambulance calls, although of course such traditional conditions as the carrying out of tradesmen's duties quickly foundered. The exception was the gallant role of the Brigade Engineers, Firemen Hector Breaks, Bill Godwin and Jock Eddie, who not only serviced the appliances, including the trailer pumps as they arrived, but provided tow bars and ladder racks for the towing vehicles. In addition to essential routine, our lads were seeing to the growing task of receiving AFS equipment, and they were responsible for the training of every AFS man and woman. The Brigade's total strength in October 1938 was 30. At the Central Fire Station, six (Deputy Chief Officer Ken Devereux, Firemen Upward, Frampton, Breaks, Dorey and Hatton) were acting as official instructors, although everyone else was similarly engaged.

During his 60-hour course, an auxiliary fireman, starting from complete ignorance of the Service, was trained in virtually every piece of a fireman's equipment and to apply himself to its use, from knots-and-lines to fire escapes, from smart parading to the use of anti-gas clothing and respirators. We ourselves were by now becoming very familiar with the identification of the expected war-time gases. These were lung irritants, blister gases, nose gases and tear gases. Streaming eyes on emerging from the gas chamber in the drill yard were a familiar sight. We were expected to recognise gases as, when and if the enemy used them, and to assist the memory, rhymes were provided. Here are two of them:

TEAR GASES

Tear Gases: First comes C.A.P.
Then K.S.K. and B.B.C.
If you smell pear drops – then beware
For K.S.K. is in the air.
These gases, to appease the mind,
Explain they really do not blind,
Remove, and re-assure you oughter
Wash out the eyes with Saline Water.

LUNG IRRITANTS

Phosgene and Chlorine are alas,
Chloropicrin too, a deadly gas,
Affects the lungs – affects the breath,
And very soon may lead to death,
The only hope is perfect rest.
Remember this and do your best.
Pop on a mask and quickly fetch her,
Without the least delay, a stretcher.
Don't let her move – give her beef tea,
Keep her as warm as she can be.
Whatever others say or think,
Don't give her alcoholic drink,
And don't, in spite of great temptation,
Try artificial respiration.

There were also rhymes on Blister Gases and Nose Gases.

In October 1938, providing space for training became a problem, and having enrolled several of their senior staff into the AFS, Bowmakers allowed part of their premises at the rear of Christchurch Road to be used. We then had 455 men undergoing training (London, incidentally, had 12,000 at that time). By December 1938, our inexhaustible Chief Officer had produced his own *Drill Book and Manual of Instruction* for the AFS.

The printers supplied 250 free copies, and the Council agreed to purchase a number, at 6d each, so that all auxiliaries might be presented with copies. And hoping against hope for a continued peace-time administration, and despite all the pressures, he submitted to the Lighting and Fire Brigade Committee on 1 September 1938 a most ambitious and comprehensive five-year Capital Expenditure Programme, which of course, became somewhat inevitably doomed.

It will be seen that, by the end of 1938, life at the Central Fire Station and the administration of the Brigade itself was now so interlocked with this new and complicated Auxiliary Fire Service that the apparent quiescence of earlier years was both dead and buried. In fact there was so much activity from the middle of that year, and thereafter, that too much detail would serve only to confuse the reader. One contended with new conditions and a new pace. We even proceeded with our now well-established annual ball at the Pavilion on 30 September 1938.

With so much acknowledgement due to our professional lads, in that they had adapted themselves so prodigiously to the intense training programme and to consistently long and laborious hours, a condition which continued for many months to come, credit was also due to many of those new auxiliaries who, by January 1939, were occupying their own stations where drilling and the learning of good firemanship continued. During the following month, no less that 48 had been promoted to the rank of Leading Fireman. Certain of them were given the additional encouragement of riding a "red appliance" with Brigade crews.

The first occasion was on 27 August 1938, when they attended a gorse fire at the rear of Bournemouth School for Boys at Strouden. The second opportunity was somewhat more spectacular.

At 8.42 pm on Friday, 9 December 1938, the concert area of Bournemouth Pier burned merrily. The Bournemouth Daily Echo reported: "Bournemouth Pier is on Fire. These almost terrifying words took scores of people out into the wild December weather last night. Flames 30 feet high, twisted into spirals by half-a-gale from the south south-west, lighted up the sky. The rain beat down mercilessly. The dancing stopped in the Pavilion ballroom, while the gaily-dressed girls and their escorts crowded to the windows giving on to the Pier Approach and watched the blaze."

Some 40 auxiliaries, who were attending a lecture at the Central Fire station, turned out and assisted in the running of 2,365 feet of hose.

On 15 May 1939, a relay exercise involving crews of auxiliaries from Pokesdown and Strouden Park (zones 3 and 8), using Beresford Stork light trailer pumps, took place at the Sheepwash, near Iford, a delightful bend in the Stour now disposed of by the diversion of the river. Section Officers Puddephatt and Cullimore were in charge and Staff Fireman Reg Westcott instructed. Auxiliary Fireman Sugarman was the source pump operator. Reg Puddephatt recalls: "After the pumping, most of us were busy shoving the intermediate pump up the slope which had become very muddy, when we heard a shout and saw Auxiliary Fireman Sugarman flapping about some yards from the bank. Auxiliary Fireman Benjamin and I jumped into the river, which was surprisingly deep, and held on to Sugarman while the rest of the crew threw us a line." Both rescuers were commended by the Council.

And the Auxiliary Fire Service personnel were by no means slow where comradeship and social activity were concerned. On 15 October 1938, a dance was organised at the Central Fire Station and a smoking concert was held at the Queen's Hall, Bath Road, now a Christadelphian Church, on 25 January 1939. This hall was a most convenient venue for quite a number of social occasions which were to be held later. By February 1939, thanks to our efforts in enrolling quite a number of well-known musicians in the town – most of Sim Grossman's Pavilion Dance Band including, for a short time, Sim himself – the AFS formed its own dance band which played at the first Bournemouth Auxiliary Fire Service (BAFS) public dance held at the Pavilion on 16 February 1939. The BAFS band extended later in such size and quality as to rival even the great Glen Miller.

During the previous month, the first copy of the AFS publication *The Fire Bucket* was produced and stencilled in our office. Edited by freelance reporter Bill Notley and Bournemouth Echo reporter George Huxtep, both having joined the AFS, it was later produced in print with considerable success, until paper shortage and the 1940 Blitz overtook us, although the Home Office had approved for official grant its free distribution to all members. Our London connections hosted a visit to their Albert Embankment headquarters by a number of our AFS personnel, plus the writer, in order to witness a most impressive display on 24 May 1939.

By the middle of February 1939, we had revised our auxiliary fireman requirements to 600, and although the Munich scare was already somewhat forgotten and a few recruits had left, we had enrolled 488. Of these, 473 were now undergoing training and 75 passed their trailer pump examination. Two first-aid courses and five anti-gas courses had been completed. The total attendance for training for the month January-February was

2,705. Ninety-five women had also been enrolled and were undergoing training. Emergency appliances were arriving, and by the end of February 1939, we had received one Sulzer Heavy pumping unit, one Large Dennis trailer pump, four Large Coventry Climax trailer pumps, one Medium Coventry Climax trailer pump and 26 Beresford Stork Light trailer pumps. These appliances were used in a demonstration at the Central Fire Station organised on behalf of the Home Office for the benefit of representatives of surrounding districts on 27 March 1939.

One thing was very clear. With 80,000 National Service leaflets having been distributed throughout the County Borough giving details of all the services, our organisation and recruitment drive was attracting much attention. The Bournemouth Times headline on 17 February 1939 announced: "Fire Brigade is best pull for National Service." It was always understood, of course, that the Air Raid Precautions department had lacked a professional base such as ours on which to build. But nevertheless, 1,486 wardens had been enrolled by 18 February 1939, plus 426 in other sections such as first aid parties, ambulance drivers, rescue parties, decontamination squads and the rest; and twenty public sirens had been ordered. Active consideration was also being given to the distribution of civilian gas masks and even to the possible accommodation of some 10,000 child evacuees.

At 4 am on Sunday, 9 July 1939, 15 counties, including Hampshire, Dorset and Wiltshire, were plunged into darkness for a blackout test, whilst aircraft flew overhead and reported results. Mr H. Barratt, the local ARP Area Controller, had stated earlier that "a light of one candle-power can be seen at a height of two miles on a clear night". Corporation workmen painted kerbs and posts white, and painted white lines on the roads.

A second blackout was scheduled for 10 August 1939, but because of bad weather, it was postponed until the following day at 4 am. However the pouring rain of the night of August 10-11 did not put off the very ambitious AFS exercise which Chief Officer Barker had so carefully organised and which was observed by Assistant Secretary of the Home Office Mr F.W.Smith, Home Office Inspector of Fire Brigades Mr Tom Breaks (our Hector Breaks's father) and the Mayor of Bournemouth. What a night it was, with 54 mock occurrences attended by the crews of all eleven zone stations, whilst I hastened the coloured mobilising pins on the wall map.

In the same month our equipment was supplemented by a further 1,000 feet of hose. A No 2 Foam-making Branch Pipe

(£29.5s) and 50 gallons of Foam Compound (at 4s per gallon) were on order scheduled for the new Leyland Dual-purpose appliance. Two single-deck buses had already been converted into Mobile Water Carriers.

Bournemouth (population 144,451, acreage 11,627 and rateable value £1,953,294) should have been a happy town in that fine summer of 1939. Until the month of August loomed, so it was, being filled almost to capacity with people on holiday. But the clouds of war were approaching fast as August advanced, and by 25 August, the station master at the Central Railway Station was being bombarded with train enquiries and a considerable exodus. On that same day, Chief Officer Barker (still constantly referred to in the local Press as "Captain Barker", which did not depress his ego) cancelled all leave "until further orders", and pumps and equipment were correctly positioned at all stations, some having been stored either at the Central Fire Station or at the Nortoft Road zone station. On 31 August, I accompanied the Chief Officer and the Chairman of the Fire Brigade Committee, now Senior Section Officer H.A.Benwell, on a close tour of inspection. In Bournemouth, sandbag filling, trench digging and shelter construction were much in evidence. Air raid shelters for 7,000 people were being prepared.

On 1 September 1939, the Germans bombed eight Polish towns by 6 am, and Warsaw itself at 9 am, and Prime Minister Chamberlain despatched an ultimatum to Hitler. General mobilisation of the Armed Forces was signed by the King. Mobilisation of the Auxiliary Fire Service was ordered by a telegram sent to all local authority fire brigades from the Home Office which announced: "Emergency Fire Brigade Measures − Call out Auxiliary Fire Service and proceed as in Circular of 23 March 1939".This circular had outlined the general requirements of a call-up, not only operationally but administratively. Throughout the country, 89,000 auxiliary firemen and 6,000 auxiliary firewomen were reporting for whole-time duty, with 14,000 emergency pumps available. In Bournemouth, we immediately called up 150 whole-time auxiliary men, 26 women and two youths. Part-time personnel, also duly alerted, numbered 600. Although only 36 emergency pumps were then in readiness, out of an allocation of 101, a further 35 were delivered within the following three weeks. And as those auxiliaries who had signified willingness for whole-time duty left their normal employment and reported to their auxiliary fire stations during the night of 1-2 September, so the rain descended. The town became alive with the sound of trailer-pumps as fifteen flood calls were responded to between 21.45 hrs. on 2 September and 01.35 hrs. on 3 September.

Bobbys, in the Square, which had suffered a roof fire on 18 February 1939, was now flooded, and lost two tons of sugar, a grocery store in Commercial Road lost a ton of provisions, several underground transformers exploded, an air-raid shelter was flooded, and even the basement of the Pier Approach Baths had to be pumped out. What a night! It was but a damp introduction to more fearful things to come.

How can one describe the multifarious arrangements which had immediately to be put in hand, although so much had been foreseen and planned? Approval was obtained for the temporary requisitioning of a further 44 towing vehicles, all requiring tow bars, and as did every other vehicle, blackout hoods for lights. Catering arrangements were made on a temporary basis with Messrs F.W. Woolworth, at a cost of 1s 4½d per head per day (the official allowance being 1s 6d). Bedding and blankets were hastily ordered and gathered, as were quantities of utensils, although much equipment was organised with keen initiative by the men of the stations. Our order was for 318 knives and forks, 174 spoons, 222 dessert spoons, 240 plates, four teapots and six kettles.

Pressure was high too in our office, for all had to be recorded and arrangements for pay and conditions of service properly organised. The pay was as follows: Section Officers, Communication Officer and Transport Officer, £4 10s per week; Auxiliary Firemen, £3 per week; and Auxiliary Firewomen £2 per week. Later, in May 1940, Leading Firemen were paid £3 5s per week. The insurance cover for AFS personnel was replaced by the provisions of the Civil (Personal) Injuries Act, which meant that the sick or injured could be discharged after two weeks. Bearing in mind that auxiliaries could leave voluntarily in any case after a notice of seven days – until service became "frozen" under the Police and Firemen's (Employment) Order 1940 in the following June – this reservation had the effect of a reduction in numbers for a while until the Government amended the Act in November 1939 and allowed sick and injury pay up to a limit of 13 weeks. All the men were on continuous duty, and the women worked an 88-hour week.

The following section officers were given charge of their crews and appliances and were accompanied by a professional fireman who acted as assistant and adviser. Each zone had its own distinguishing sign (in parenthesis) which was displayed on its vehicles. Zone 1 – A.N. Matthewson with Fireman Pete

Dorey (Rectangle); Zone 2 – R. Preston with Fireman Pat Davis (Cross); Zone 3 – R. W. Puddephatt with Fireman Bill Baker (Triangle); Zone 4 – J. Wainman with Fireman Reg Westcott (Clover Leaf); Zone 5 – R.G.L. Fisher with Fireman Harry Andrews (Diamond); Zone 6 – J.H. Akhurst with Fireman Frank Breeze (Horseshoe); Zone 7 – T.I. Pearmain with Fireman Harold Smith (Heart); Zone 8 – T.W. Bevan with Fireman Theo Janku (Pennant); Zone 9 – M.P. Austing with Fireman George Cooper (Star); Zone 10 – H. Cullimore with Fireman Dick Law (Axe); Zone 11 – G. Barber with Fireman Arthur Linter (Circle). Mr N. Willoughby was appointed Communications Officer with Fireman Tom Upward as his assistant, and Mr B.E. Nicholls as Transport Officer. Canon Hedley Burrows, vicar of St Peter's, became our Honorary Chaplain. Councillor H.A. Benwell was appointed Commandant (unpaid) of the Bournemouth Auxiliary Fire Service. Of the professional Brigade, Deputy Chief Officer Ken Devereux was posted at the Town Hall as Liaison Officer with Air Raid Precautions, Station Officer Joe Thackwray assumed the rank of Deputy Chief Officer in Ken Devereux's absence, Sub-Officer Ivor Bolt (promoted on 28 August 1939, with an increased wage of £4 rising to £5, following success in the IFE examinations) was in charge of uniform, anti-gas clothing and respirators, Fireman Hector Breaks had charge of pumps and Fireman Arthur Hatton had charge of hose.

Important to decision making was the formation of a Fire Brigade Emergency Committee, being a sub-committee of the Lighting and Fire Brigade Committee of the Council, which had "power to act" and whose members were to make themselves available at any time. This committee consisted of Councillors H.A. Benwell (Chairman), Walter C. Street (vice-chairman), J.E. Bevis, E. Richards and R.F. Seward.

Then it was Sunday, 3 September 1939. Chief Officer William Howard Barker and I stood in his office on that fateful morning. We listened in silence to Prime Minister Chamberlain's voice on the radio: "This morning, the British Ambassador in Berlin handed the German Government a final note stating that, unless we heard from them by 11 o'clock that they were prepared at once to withdraw their troops from Poland, a state of war would exist between us. I have to tell you now that no such undertaking has been received and that, consequently, this country is at war with Germany."

Despite months of warning and preparation, we were struck dumb, until the Chief strolled slowly into the drill yard and looked skywards. When would it all start? In Bournemouth all cinemas, theatres and football grounds were closed by Government order but in two weeks they were allowed to re-open provided that all entertainments ceased by 10 pm. As a Brigade, our organisation of the Bournemouth Auxiliary Fire Service, under the purposeful direction of Chief Officer Barker was, from what we heard from other parts of the country, second to none. Yet there was still much to be done and priority begat priority. Additional telephones were installed, as was emergency lighting at the Central Fire Station, and 1,000 fireproof identity discs were ordered.

As all the stations had need of a great deal of sandbagging. both bags and sand had to be requisitioned before those very weighty objects were heaved into place. A framework of timber and corrugated iron filled with sand protected both control room and offices at the Central Fire station, behind which the passageway was christened the "Polish Corridor", this being the current description of Germany's route into that unfortunate country. A great deal of discomfort was, and continued to be, taken for granted. The common catch-phrase was: "Don't you know there's a war on?" Some "had it made", as at Zone 10 (Strouden Park Hotel); others not so, such as the "Barker Boys' Dump" at Maxwell Road Corporation Depot, which they shared with dust carts, 24 cart-horses and myriads of flies. And in the midst of everything, drills and exercises were the order of the day, and often the night. Our one fatal accident occurred on 6 October 1939 when Auxiliary Leading Fireman Reg Cooper tragically slipped under the wheels of a moving AFS van outside No 7 (Nortoft Road) station, during an exercise. Driver Frank Miles, who later joined the professionals, never forgot that terrible moment.

AFS: badge of the Auxiliary Fire Service, 1938-41.

AFS 7: spearheading the recruitment poster, 1939.

Auxiliary Fire Service: hose-training, supervised by staff fireman Pat Davis at Zone No.2 fire station (Palmerston Road, Boscome), 1939.

Auxiliary Fire Service: sandbagged blast-walls being built around Zone No.5 fire station (Maxwell Road, Winton), 1939.

The Phoney War – Bournemouth prepares

A full-scale exercise was held on Sunday, 24 February 1940, which embraced practically the whole of the Southern Region. For its purpose, it was assumed that Southampton, Gosport, Portsmouth and Slough had been bombed. Bournemouth sent crews from Zones 5, 6 and 7 to complete a total of 62 pumps. One of the highlights was the mobile water exercise, which included 23 vehicles each carrying 1,000 gallons of water. On 17 March 1940, two old cottages, opposite Strouden Nurseries – close to the present Castle Lane-Wessex Way roundabout – were set alight, having been well and truly fuelled. Auxiliary firemen from five zone stations worked from a 1,000 gallon dam. A local mobilising exercise followed at 6 am on 12 April, which was designed to test the patrol system and which, later that day, developed into a regional scheme exercise, bringing in both Poole and Christchurch AFS.

Throughout the Emergency Fire Brigade Scheme, the importance of establishing emergency water supplies occupied a great deal of attention, as no one doubted that, during any kind of concentrated air attack, the water mains were likely to be rendered useless.

By March 1940 we had listed a number of such supplies including the Pier Approach Baths with 150,000 gallons; Stokewood Road Baths, 92,000 gallons; an underground tank at the Russell-Cotes Art Gallery, 10,000 gallons; Castle Road Laundry (which also had an artesian well capable of providing 3,500 gallons per hour), 27,000 gallons; Queen's Park pond, 367,000 gallons; Coy Pond, 360,000 gallons. There were various hotel swimming pools, such at Cotford Hall, 20,000 gallons; the Majestic Hotel, 10,000 gallons, and Linden Hall, 14,000 gallons. The Pavilion fountain contained 48,000 gallons and the Pavilion's own pumping plant was of considerable capacity. Elevated tanks at the Corporation's East Yard and at Meyrick Park were considered less reliable. Sumps were being constructed in the Bourne stream and there were other artesian wells at Malmesbury and Parsons' Dairies, Palmerston Road, and at the South Western Mineral Company, Spring Road. There was also the Alderney reservoir which held 12,000,000 gallons. Six steel Supplementary Water Supply (SWS) dams, each containing 5,000 gallons, were erected at the Imperial Hotel (Lansdowne), Avenue Road Car Park, J.J. Allens (Seamore Road), Hendy's Garage (Palmerston Road), the Richmond Hotel (Charminster) and the Winton Library. The mains system was minutely studied, including the salt water supplies.

The months which followed the outbreak of war produced a strange atmosphere of anti-climax in what seemed a long period of "phoney war". There were no bombs, until the first fell on Canterbury on 9 May 1940, and nothing much other than expectancy on the Western Front as Hitler shared out Poland with his newly-found and temporary Russian friends. This was most certainly a time for consolidation and the building up of arms for the Armed Forces and pumps and equipment for the Fire Service. In fact, bearing in mind that only 60 percent of the Government's estimated requirement of emergency pumps were available on 1 September 1939, this breathing space was heaven-sent, and no fewer than 500 pumps were manufactured and delivered each week until May 1940. The eventual number of pumps supplied nationally totalled 26,300 costing £4,376,222. Bournemouth had received 80 pumps by the end of September 1939. The number of auxiliary firemen varied during those early months, a few leaving to join the Armed Forces, being bored by a seeming lack of purpose and by the inadequate conditions. By January 1940, our number of whole-time auxiliaries had been reduced to 145 (124 firemen and 21 officers – Deputy Section Officers now being appointed), plus 22 firewomen. The part-timers numbered 431. There was indeed a negative side to the period of apparent enemy inaction and members of the public were complaining of the "waste of money" and describing our Service as "the darts brigade".

The effect was felt more by the local Civil Defence Organisation, a review of which was being undertaken nationally by the Government in October 1939. There were harsh exchanges therefore when, at the January 1940 meeting of the Council, an increase of 35 men for the AFS was requested, and remarks questioned the resourcefulness of Chief Officer Barker. Ever in his defence, Councillor Benwell stated: "I want to say that it is entirely wrong for some people to say that it is because of the influence of our Chief Officer that we have such an elaborate scheme in Bournemouth."

Perhaps that was with half-a-tongue in his cheek. After all, the Home Office were requiring a first-line turnout of 25 pumps which necessitated the extra personnel, and operational men were now enjoying one day off every six days. We were now having to buy towing vehicles instead of merely borrowing them; we had just ordered 700 rubber waterproof coats, at 17s 6d each, leggings for our messengers and the much-required haversacks for our respirators (gas masks). Chief Officer Bill

Ballance of Poole told of the dear old lady who, when it was suggested that we might not be bombed after all, exclaimed: "What, and after all this expense on the rates!"

As far as the Bournemouth professionals were concerned, this almost cataclysmic activity had, rather sadly, brought about an unsought degree of fragmentation. Elsewhere, particularly in London, the regulars – a term used to describe the professionals – reacted quite strongly against having to share their stations and indeed their established profession with this great army of outsiders. This was not so in Bournemouth, as from the start, we accepted a situation which was inevitable, and encouraged by a general sense of good nature, we plunged into our new and extensive work and responsibility. It might also be noted that our own ranks had been swelled by newcomers who were brought in to strengthen and develop the Brigade itself. Some were officially on a temporary basis, as Chief Officer Barker had taken advantage of his emergency powers and his association with the Fire Brigades Division. These lads arrived only after the EFBO scheme was put into operation, and included Bill Godwin (4/7/38), Jock Eddie and Theo Janku (24/8/38), Frank Breeze and Harold Smith (17/10/38), Pat Davis (16/1/39), Bert Radford (18/8/39), Jim Collingbourne and Vic House (2/5/40), Frank Miles and George Fairbrother – the latter transferred from Harrow (1/7/40). The extraordinary change of life in the Bournemouth Fire Brigade was therefore so much more dramatic for those of us who were weaned on truly peace-time conditions.

The Bournemouth regulars were by no means the favoured ones, and it would not be untrue or unfair to declare that our efforts were rewarded with little thanks. For instance, the Council decided in February 1940 to discontinue paying our instructors of the AFS their bonus of five shillings per week because "the instruction could now be continued on the zone stations". This was despite the fact that so much responsibility for instruction on those stations lay in the hands of members of our professional Brigade who received no compensation whatsoever. On 15 August 1940, we asked for a war bonus of five shillings per week for all our men, which though being agreed by the Emergency Committee, was promptly turned down by the Council. After further pressure, however, and the great blitz period, it was eventually agreed in February 1941.

There were rewards for some. Honoraria were presented in April 1939 to the Chief Officer (£50), the Deputy Chief Officer (£25) and the Station Officer (£10). The Chief Officer's salary was advanced to its maximum of £500 on 1 April 1940, he having applied for the firemaster's office at Glasgow the previous month, and having also just received an increased travel allowance of £75 per annum. Sadly that kindly and loveable old veteran Joe Frampton, so recently training the AFS in the drill yard, became worn out and ill, and died on 7 April 1940 after 27 years of unstinted service. He was one of the old Brigade's true gentlemen. His widow was ushered from her Cotlands Road flat with undisguised haste and eventually granted a gratuity of £40, under Section 262 of the Bournemouth Corporation Act, in June 1940.

In February 1940, George Cooper, after so recently entering the Brigade, received a rank in the Wembley Brigade, Tommy Upward moved to Tottenham Brigade in the following month and Hector Breaks to Leicester City Brigade in June 1940. Later, in February 1941, Jock Eddie's request to transfer to Derby was turned down, although he and Bill Godwin were given a little recognition (2s 6d and 5s per week respectively) of their invaluable maintenance of pumps and vehicles, in June 1940.

In January 1940, a letter signed by members of the Brigade asked for consideration to be given to the upgrading of sick and injury pay. This was referred to the Finance Committee which took no action. By October 1940, we again registered the fact that, although the AFS had received some consideration concerning accidents, our sick and injury pay arrangements had not been revised despite war conditions. The Council, at its meeting on 31 October, instructed the Town Clerk to make enquiries of insurance companies in that respect. It was not until 10 April 1941 that it was announced that we were to receive sick pay conditions on a par with the Auxiliary Fire Service.

In December 1940, both the professionals and members of the AFS, many having been tried in all the violence of blitz conditions, felt deserving of a little more off-duty time than the prevailing one day in six, and through the medium of the Fire Brigades Union, an application was made, which was "referred back" by the Council on 16 January 1941 pending enquiries with other Brigades. On 13 February 1941, a deputation consisting of Harry Short (Assistant General Secretary of the Fire Brigades Union), Peter Dorey (now sub-officer), AFS Leading Fireman Ron Harding and AFS Fireman Pretty met the Fire Brigade Committee, which bowed to Chief Officer Barker's recommendation that no further leave could be entertained until the whole-time establishment could be increased. He had already applied to the Home Office for an increase of twenty-five men. Success came, however, when all whole-time men were granted one day off in four in April 1941.

On 10 May 1940, Hitler marched into Holland, having already conquered Scandinavia during April and May, and the real war began. For us, all leave was cancelled once again and no fire service personnel were allowed outside the County Borough. France's so-called Maginot Line was by-passed and overrun, as were the allied troops who, by the end of that month, were either gunned down, captured or being rescued from across the Channel by craft of all descriptions. Three trips were made by the *Massey Shaw*, London's famous fireboat which brought back 96 men and transferred 500 to other ships. 300,000 troops were rescued from the beaches of Dunkirk.

Bournemouth was on the receiving end of 20,000 French and Belgian soldiers, an unforgettable sight of these men who had been forced to flee from hell. The writer is reminded of the occasion when, in the course of chatting to a couple of "poilu" by Bournemouth Pier, he invited them to partake of a trip in the bay by way of the Brigade's 14 feet outboard-powered dinghy. They came, but another roll on the waves was hardly an answer to their plight.

The beaches were available for some weeks, until the piers were blown up on 5 July. It seemed that parachute landings were more to be expected, and as early as 1 June, all road signs were removed. Looking back, the picture of scores of armed Jerries dropping in and creating a bridgehead might look a trifle over-dramatic, but the vulnerability of our South Coast was very real indeed. The Brigade placed 24-hour virtually unarmed guards on all the entrances to our fire stations – for what use they would have been. Commandant Benwell, in his wisdom, wrote to the Home Secretary: "Many of us are ex-service men and we all realise the new dangers that beset us due to enemy troops landing by aeroplane. You have, in every town and village, a well-disciplined body of men, and if they were armed, you have a very good line of defence . . . I realise that this would probably mean placing the AFS under military authorities, but I see no difficulty here at all."

Sir John Anderson's secretary replied: "Your letter shall have attention." Our minds boggled!

Even before the great air onslaught began, conditions seem so remote and unreal in restrospect. How, for instance, were we able to drive during the years of blackout without serious accident, for the light emerging from the screened headlamps was incredibly dim? I was invariably alerted from my desk to drive the Chief Officer to incidents, and also to and from his Masonic lodge. Despite petrol rationing, life continued on the roads, as did fire and ambulance calls. In March 1940, the order dated September 1932, which permitted drivers to proceed against traffic signals and one-way traffic routes was cancelled. Finding addresses with all the windows blacked out and with no street lighting was, let us say, a little disconcerting at times. Yet this unparalleled situation (First World War conditions were not so drastic) lifted the rigidity of convention and brought about a spirit of co-operation which the post-war years have never hoped to reclaim. During the war, anyone could cadge a lift without question or apprehension.

Trailer-pumps: massed ranks of Coventry Climax units (left) and Beresford Storks (centre and right-hand lines) on arrival at the Central Fire Station, Bournemouth, in 1939.

Beresford Stork: trailer-pump and her Auxiliary Fire Service crew (Firemen Loram, Kaile, Brocklesby and Young) from No.7 Zone fire station (Nortoft Road, Charminster). Stork and handlers would go together to many blitzed towns in 1940-41.

OPPOSITE – Training flames: a derelict thatched cottage is put to the torch, near Castle Lane, on 17 March 1940

We could lose the war by Fire! Be ready for FIREBOMB FRITZ!

We could lose the war by fire! *We could. But we WON'T.*
We of Britain's Fire Guard will see to that.
Fire Guard work is often dull. Sometimes its dangerous.
But it's work that's *got* to be done. So we put into it
every ounce of enthusiasm we've got. We watch un-
ceasingly! We train till we're *really* good! We know all
the awkward places, and how to get there. We won't be
caught off guard as Firebomb Fritz will find.

BRITAIN SHALL NOT BURN!

ISSUED BY THE MINISTRY OF HOME SECURITY

Bournemouth's first bomb: destroys a house in Cellar's Farm Road, on the cliffs at Southbourne, hit at 00.12 hours on 3 July 1940.

OPPOSITE – Firebomb Fritz: leaflet from the Ministry of Home Security warning of incendiary bombs in 1940; weighing a kilo, these had a core of aluminium iron oxide encased in magnesium alloy.

Air Raid Warnings 'Red', Jerry overhead – Bournemouth hit

The Luftwaffe lost no time in establishing itself on French airfields, and by the middle of June, they commenced to bomb and strafe our own fighter bases. In the early morning of 19 June 1940, Southampton received its first visit by the enemy, and whilst Bournemouth had its first "Red Alert" between the hours of 02.00 and 03.00, we despatched several crews to Southampton for standby duty. The south coast was beginning to get used to its "Air Raid Warning – Yellow" signals as circulated by the RAF to indicate a standby. This would normally precede a "Red Alert" and the presence of enemy aircraft, then the "moaning minnie" sirens would wail, and shelter was indicated. There were occasions, of course, when Jerry would pop across the Channel without warning being given. Apart from local bombing, "Yellows" and "Reds" were nightly occurrences for many months to come as we listened to the drone of engines above us. It was so often in via Bournemouth and out by the same route, as the Swastika-marked Luftwaffe flew on its horrendous errand to the West, the Midlands and the North. Often its planes would drop any spare luggage as our coast was reached on the homeward journey, mostly on the beach or in the sea, and the vibration would shake the town.

On Red Alerts, pump crews from the various zone stations would proceed to action stations situated on their various routes. Stand-by periods were often long, cold and wearisome as Jerry's return was awaited. Such an action station was situated in Queens Park, from whence a well-known Bournemouth councillor invited the crews to his kitchen for hot tea, usually brought in by an attractive maid. One night an auxiliary fireman, boasting of his amorous intent, grabbed the bearer of the tray as she entered and kissed her enthusiastically. It was the councillor's wife!

An action station situated at a certain pub in Holdenhurst Road housed its delectable barmaids. There another adventurous fireman, assisted by others of his crew, climbed a ladder to the girls' bedroom. Nearing the top, he was greeted by the contents of a chamber-pot and was thereafter duly christened and avoided at the mess table.

The inevitable happened at 00.12 hours on 3 July 1940, when a solitary high-explosive bomb was dropped on a house in Cellars Farm Road, Southbourne, setting it well alight and so presenting our Brigade with the real thing. Altogether 19 properties were damaged. Deputy Chief Ken Devereux with ten staff firemen attended in our two dual-purpose appliances, supported by seven AFS men from Zone 10.

Miss Eglington, who occupied the house with her father, mother and three evacuee boys, told the press "There was an explosion and the next we knew was the wall falling down. We ran downstairs and have lost everything. As we went, water came through the ceiling and later fire broke out in the roof. Our three cats, a bird and a goldfish were unharmed. We were of course stunned by the shock but none of us was injured. I'm off to work today as usual."

On that same day, as Greta Garbo charmed us in "Ninochka" at the Carlton Cinema, as the Russians poured into Romania, and as Britons were being evacuated from Hong Kong to Singapore, so our Odeon audiences were enjoying Bing Crosby and Bob Hope in "The Road to Singapore".

The anticipated air attacks were undoubtedly upon us and protection for our stations and personnel was now being reinforced. At the Central Fire Station, conditions were somewhat makeshift and use was made of additionally-timbered basement rooms in two Cotlands Road flats, including mine. In August 1940, arrangements were made to build an overground shelter in what was then the Citax Taxi Park, at the rear of our workshops.

On 9 August at 23.24 hours, the dual-purpose appliance from Central, accompanied by AFS crews from Zones 9 and 11, was called to 47, Alyth Road, which had been demolished by a high-explosive bomb. A Mrs Thornley was at the point of leaving her bedroom when her house fell about her and she remained buried under debris for about an hour.

Fortunately there was no fire as Staff Fireman Pat Davis and his crew cut their way through to her and so freed that rather unclad lady. Our Pat was patted on the back by Chief Officer Barker and the Chairman of the Fire Brigade Committee, but his only memento was a boot polish tin lid, inscribed and beribboned, which was presented by his lads back at the station. In a letter to the Bournemouth Echo, a lady wrote of the protection afforded by "putting one's head under the pillow".

At 06.30 hours on the following day, five high-explosive bombs were dropped on Meon Road, damaging 38 houses and killing a passing cyclist. There were remarkable personal escapes, and one explosion for instance threw a lawn mower a distance of a hundred yards. During August, 23 such bombs were dropped during a total of seven raids on Alyth Road,

Huntley Road, Keswick Road, Chessel Avenue, Beechwood Avenue, West Howe, Wicklea Road and High Howe Lane. In addition, 30 incendiary bombs landed on Iford and Tuckton and a petrol bomb was also dropped. Madison Road and Walpole Road were machine-gunned, and one of our Spitfires, with Pilot Officer Cecil Henry Hight of New Zealand, was shot down and crashed in Walsford Road on 15 August. The lad perished. With 248 properties damaged in those six weeks of 1940, it was amazing that only one civilian was killed and thirteen others injured.

The reader will appreciate that the concern of the Brigade and the Fire Service generally at all of the enemy-action incidents was primarily that of actual fire or the imminent possibility of fire, and much was left in the good hands of the First Aid, Rescue, Police and other services. It is hardly possible to record detail of the 52 local enemy-action incidents,which finally ended on 27 May 1944. Yet let it be here recorded that, in addition to enemy action, the Brigade was called to attend no fewer than 594 normal incidents during the period 3 September 1939 to 18 August 1941, when the National Fire Service took over. Such calls responded to during the crucial year of 1940 numbered 342. The Bournemouth Fire Brigade, one way or another, was kept rather busy.

There were many periods during the war that remain ever imprinted on the mind. August 1940 saw air battles in the sky over Bournemouth day after day. It was an astonishing sight, 367 miles-per-hour Spitfires and Hurricanes weaving around, breaking up the enemy's tremendous formation and with vapour trails and bursts of smoke appearing like feathered whisps against an azure backcloth. On 11 August, 61 enemy aircraft were shot down over the south of England. The following day 61 more, and on 13 August, 78 met their fate. On 15 August, when we visited the wreck of the Spitfire in Walsford Road, 144 of the enemy were destroyed. German formations continued to fly over us during September and October.

On 25 September, a single Heinkel 111 bomber was seen diving in flames over Branksome. Of the three airmen who baled out, one was found dead on a railway embankment, another was dead on the beach, whilst the third was rescued from the sea. The plane sat squarely on the ruins of "Underwood", Westminster Road. Chief Officer Barker and I watched as the dead pilot, clearly visible, was consumed in the flames. During his search for souvenirs, Barker found a machine-gun, which he brought back to his office, from which it was officially

78

removed some days later.

During September 1940, 21 high-explosives, one petrol bomb, one oil bomb and a number of incendiaries destroyed three properties and damaged 391 others, whilst killing seven people and injuring 17 at Seabourne Road, Southville Road, Christchurch Road, Surrey Road South, Burnaby Road, Durley Chine, Hawkwood Road, Crabton Close Road, Westminster Road, Holdenhurst and Throop. A repaired Dornier 17 bomber was on view to the public at Dean Park during the summer of 1940. 10,000 people eventually visited it and the "one shilling to view" was contributed to Bournemouth's Spitfire Fund. October brought only three bomb incidents when a total of 15 high-explosives were dropped, injuring 14 people and damaging 288 properties. In five raids during November, the Luftwaffe delivered 24 high-explosive bombs, 6 parachute mines and a number of incendiaries, which killed 62 people, injured 132, and damaged 2,829 properties.

The worst of these November raids was on the night of 16 November at 3.30 hours, when parachute mines fell on Alma Road School and in St Leonards Road, Malmesbury Park Road, Westbourne, and Turbery Common. High-explosive bombs and incendiaries dropped on Knyveton Road, Gervis Road East, Meyrick Road, Groveley Manor, Terrace Road, Leven Avenue, Montague Road and Southern Road.

Ted Amey remembers the night of the parachute mines, in fact the early morning of 16 November. His station at Nortoft Road was in the centre of devastation, so near to St Leonards Road and Malmesbury Park Road, where fifty people were killed and a large number injured. He and his colleagues were caught up in a considerable rescue operation and there were such scenes as are "better not remembered". Both the Rescue Services and the AFS received high praise for their work and heroism during those fateful hours. One of the six mines completely destroyed Alma Road school as the writer's mother watched from her garden gate. Meanwhile, fire crews were concentrating upon Westbourne, where about 400 incendiary bombs were dropped.

There was only one incident in December, when on the 21st, high-explosives dropped on Old Bridge Road and Castle Lane damaged 21 properties. Much of this death, injury and destruction was due to "sheddings" from the devastating raids which other towns and cities were suffering. From the tower in the Central Fire Station yard we could see the glow in the sky as Southampton, 30 miles away, burned. As early as 13 August, that great town was aflame around the old docks for some two weeks, and the High Street was blocked for longer. Then came September, October and even worse in November, when five Southampton firemen were killed on the 23rd, and on the 30th a raid in which 120 planes delivered 800 bombs and killed 137 people, and which brought in fire service reinforcements amounting to 2,000 men and 160 pumps.

The air raids of the summer of 1940 were obviously the precursor of an intense effort by Hitler to force the collapse of our country by sheer devastation, not only of our wherewithal to fight back but of towns and cities, where, it was anticipated, the morale of the population would collapse. It is a story which will have been read and viewed on television many times. Can one be forgiven for hoping that the terrors and imbecility of war have imprinted themselves upon even the youngest of minds, that the world might advance from the influence of both national and international vandals and of the wiles of the clever but unwise? History will never omit the events of the autumn and winter of 1940, nor must it ever play down the ravages of uncontrolled fire caused by human will, or the sheer guts and heroism of the firemen who fought that terror on the ground. Stories have been related by those who were much more witness than the writer, who endeavours only, and with comparative brevity, to transmit a little of what was once the Bournemouth Fire Brigade and the Bournemouth Auxiliary Fire Service. Let us indeed be reminded of the part played by our local lads in the blitz areas mostly from September 1940, throughout 1941 and then more occasionally up to 1944.

OPPOSITE, top – an engine in the kitchen: 'Mrs Drew (left) and Mrs Seaton just escaped death when an enemy plane crashed on their house on Sunday. Engine of the raider is in the foreground of this picture taken in the burned out kitchen.' That week the Bournemouth Times also recorded the funeral of rescue worker William Henry Vaughan.

OPPOSITE, bottom – abseiling: smiles of achievement as the Auxiliary Fire Service comes down to earth at No.8 Zone fire station (Pelhams, Kinson) in 1940; note the blast-wall in front of the window.

Drew (left) and Mrs. Seaton
escaped death when an enemy
crashed on their house on Sun-
Engine of the raider is in the
round of this picture taken in
urned out kitchen.

Bournemouth Firemen – Blitz heroes

September 7 brought the start of the London blitz, when an attack was made by 600 German planes, and during that month the London Fire Service suffered 50 firemen killed and 500 injured. In December, when London was set ablaze by incendiary bombs and no fewer than 2,600 pumps were at work, 14 firemen were slaughtered by the Luftwaffe and 200 were injured. That was the occasion when Hermann Goering boasted: "This is the historic hour when our Air Force for the first time delivered its stroke right into the heart of the enemy."

Notwithstanding the apparent limitation of a fire service based upon local control, communication between the Government, the regions, and fire authorities was well established with respect to those which were reasonably alert and well-organised. With Chief Officer Barker's prepared relationships, it was small wonder that Bournemouth should be the first provincial town to send reinforcements to London, and from October 1940, to exchange crews with our capital city in order that its weary heroes might take a rest. On 19 October, 40 Bournemouth auxiliaries, led by Deputy Chief Officer Ken Devereux, left for London, and a similar number of their lads arrived in Bournemouth. The understanding was that the periods concerned were on a weekly basis but some of our crews remained in London for two weeks. Our Chief Officer decided that his professional men should not be denied this experience, and most of them, often two at a time, accompanied the AFS men who, on later occasions, travelled in a single-decker bus which had been acquired for such a purpose.

War is often a strange phenomenon. As men rushed to be called up for battle, so firemen strove to get to the blitz areas. Some cut cards for the privilege of going to fight in these often relentless conditions, and it was reported that a certain AFS Leading Fireman offered his mate half-a-crown to be allowed to take his place in London. Another interesting phenomenon, best explained as an insight into the mind and nature of man, is seen in a reluctance by those once involved in so much action to re-think, let alone resurrect, memories of even the most profound experiences. Of the few who, five decades later, are still with us, some have thought fit not to open their stored subconscious past. Others laughingly joke: "Oh, I really have nothing to tell." Yet on being persuaded, they unfold quite astonishing dramas.

Deputy Section Officer Jack Pike, after being on duty much of the night during a raid on Bournemouth, found himself in London at 7 a.m., when a stick of bombs fell across his allocated station and he was in action within five minutes.

Undoubtedly Bournemouth's most talented and best-loved dance-band musician, as well as a formidable veteran member of the Bournemouth Golf Club, Jack Dunkley was a blitz fireman. With inimitable and infectious humour, he told of one of his many London experiences. He was a member of probably the first crew to go there. He relates: "I was on a flat roof, accompanied by 'Curly' (Les) Downer." He was another well-known local golfer. "We were playing our jets into MacDougalls in the Milwall Dock area. It was in September and Jerry was coming in in waves" – 375 bombers and fighters were engaged – "and they were following the river. As they approached so the ack-ack followed their course. There was a hell of a noise. Suddenly I found myself falling, and landing on the pavement, and found myself relatively unhurt as 'Bene' " – Commandant Benwell was in London on five occasions – "sprang up from nowhere and asked if I was all right. My immediate thought was for 'Curly', for the fire was now underneath him, and luckily he came down safely."

Eddie Elgar remembers the great fires also at the Millwall Docks, which he modestly referred to as a "fifty-pump job". He was also among the first swap with the London firemen and his crew were stationed at Bow. Ted Amey was in the thick of the warehouse and dock fires and was stationed in London's Commercial Road.

Stationed at Wapping, yet another AFS gallant, who later served his post-war years as a professional, was Ken Brocklesby, whose memory of the East India Docks conflagration is vivid. He drove into the area with chaos all around, fires everywhere, electric wires sparking across the road and people screaming. As he manoeuvred his vehicle and trailer pump between the craters, he recalls a land-mine dropping close by, showering his crew with debris. He stood upon what was once a door for some time before discovering that beneath it was the body of a man. In a crater nearby lay the remains of a trailer pump. He was in London for two weeks and attended a number of incidents including a blazing block of flats. London Brigade was working a 48 hours on – 24 hours off system of duty at that time, which delighted our one-day-off-in-six Bournemouth lads, and being off duty, Ken decided to visit Madame Tussauds, only to be ushered out when an unexploded bomb landed nearby.

The London blitz went on and on. The first night without a raid for fifty-seven nights was 3 November 1940. This was followed by a non-stop dusk-to dawn raid on 5/6 November. Our lads were there. One of our professionals, Dick Law, spent 14 days and nights in London, together with fellow-professional Basil Stocks, and was stationed at a school in Dulwich. He tells of being surrounded by fire in the great City blitz on the night of 29 December 1940, when it was estimated that some 100,000 incendiaries were dropped during a period of three hours – seeking to wipe out London's commercial centre. All around St Paul's Cathedral was holocaust, and many are the stories of the famous Redcross Street Fire Station which, itself alight, was rescued by its own crew and remained an island in a great area of devastation for some time afterwards. Ron Harding spent a week at that station and the writer stayed there for a night after the blitz period. Dick also tells of the monstrous noise of the ack-ack guns, as even the ships on the river opened up on the waves of enemy planes. It was, incidentally, the deliberately chosen occasion by the enemy when a low tide meant that the river as a water supply was inaccessible, and in addition, an initial fall of high-explosives had fractured twelve of the largest water mains. A night to remember! Nor will London forget its biggest raid, on 19 March 1941, when 500 planes attacked, leaving 750 dead and starting 1,800 fires.

It was on the night of 22 November 1940 that a request for a reinforcement to speed to Birmingham came through. Being a fellow ex-Brummy, the writer sought permission to be included, a request to which the Chief Officer assented but to which Fire Brigade Committee Chairman Benwell dissented (well, admin could hardly be shut down at that time). But Chief Officer Barker and 25 men, including yet another ex-Brummy, Jack Dunkley, departed and stayed for a week, helping to sort out the chaos caused not only by Jerry but also by that city's poor organisation.

Both Eddie Elgar and Ted Amey were stationed at Winston Green and attended fires in various parts of that Midland metropolis, including areas around the Bull Ring. With mains fractures, much of the water supply was relayed from canals, and Ken Brocklesby spent much time on a barge in charge of four Sulzer pumps secured thereon. Jack Dunkley also spent time pumping into relays from a barge. Some of our lads were billeted in an asylum building, and had their legs pulled about it on their return home.

As previously mentioned, Southampton was a fairly constant

target for enemy bombing and strafing, being conveniently located just across the Channel, and crews and pumps from Bournemouth were often in action. Several veterans have described the amazing scene whereby thousands of people were met walking wearily along the Lyndhurst Road and into the New Forest. "It was just like the crowds one sees emerging from a big football match," said one old wartime fireman, as he told of the almost nightly evacuation of that city suffering its thunderous assault.

The rendezvous, during the early occasions, was Fire Brigade Headquarters at St Mary's Road and the problem was how to reach that point through the huge amount of debris, craters and hanging tram wires. Eddie Elgar worked on the remains of Edwin Jones's store and other large properties at that end of the town. He was also at Ranks Flour Mill on the docks on 30 November 1940.

Ron Harding has cause to remember that terrible night. He smiles now as he tells of climbing the stairs of Ranks, during that six-hour raid, and becoming involved in a huge explosion which turned out to be the result of dust ignition. As the high-explosives fell, he and his crew climbed under a railway truck, and minutes after they left that cover the whole train was blown up. One hundred and sixty pumps were at work that night. Ted Amey's crew finally reached St Mary's Road, via Bassett, after extinguishing many incendiaries on the way. He recalls the docks and the whole town area in flames. He worked on a timber yard at Northam Bridge and had to rely on tidal water, the mains having been destroyed.

Gordon Kaile has vivid memories of Southampton too. The little old lady who, emerging from a shelter, was asked, "Why do you insist on staying here?" "Because," she replied, "this is where I was born and this is where I stay."

At the end of Southampton's blitz ordeal, it was estimated that 2,361 high-explosive and 31,000 incendiary bombs killed 630 people and injured 1,877.

Like Southampton, Portsmouth was bombed repeatedly – five times during the second week of March 1941 – and again our Bournemouth lads, with their pumps, saw some real action. Deputy Chief Ken Devereux returned and told of how he watched helplessly as incendiaries pitched on the roof of the Guildhall, setting it alight. Eddie Elgar was there that night with a crew of three, driving Bournemouth's mobile dam. The assembly point was at Fareham, where shrapnel dropped from the sky. Eddie was also at Gosport dealing with a great shower of incendiaries, one of which bounced off a roof on to the neck of a warden and killed him. At Gosport, Ted Amey attended the oil tanks which were well ablaze, and Jack Dunkley spent his time there cooling down the remaining tanks. Ron Harding and his crew pumped from the sea in the precincts of HMS *Vernon*. In the morning, having feasted lavishly from the Navy's well-stocked larder, he went to investigate the progress of his relay and found that the next pump and its crew had long since departed for home, leaving his water supply to run freely away.

The blitz bombing of the provinces developed more in early 1941, and so it was with both Portsmouth and Plymouth. Both of these towns had Police Fire Brigades and Plymouth in particular suffered a very neglected auxiliary organisation. On 20 and 21 March 1941, that town was devastated by two raids in which 250 Luftwaffe bombers took part. High-explosive bombs were dropped on the fires and there was machine-gunning. Len Bailey, an old professional colleague, writes: "I remember seeing the city centre in ruins, complete devastation, one could not recognise the buildings, be they banks, shops or blocks of offices. It reminded me of the pictures of ancient Babylon."

Eddie Elgar's convoy met, as at Southampton, thousands of people trudging away from the holocaust. He describes how he saw planes diving down between the barrage balloons, and one bomber being blown up in the air, having been hit by an ack-ack shell. Whilst his crew was diverted from an assembly point at Burnham-on-Sea, Ted Amey was sent in from Taunton and both he and Ken Brocklesby worked on the rescue of cart horses which, being both petrified and burnt, were released from the stables of the Great Western Railway yard. Ken remembers seeing human bodies half-covered by sheets of tin. Eddie Elgar recalls: "We relieved a Plymouth crew and took over a Beresford Stork pump in the main road. There was fire everywhere but we soon got two delivery lines going and we were the only pump in action as far as we could see. When daylight came, we found several bodies in the debris of a shop which had received a direct hit, and we informed the local rescue team of the ARP, who removed four dead, three male and one female. We also heard that a crew from Newquay who were down the road from us had been killed by falling masonry in the block of flats they were working on."

Jack Dunkley's crew worked on the Co-op building and was helped all night by a lone sailor who, it later transpired, was charged by the Navy with desertion for his trouble. Several of these modest heroes tell of the kindness of the public, of the

Voluntary Services, of nuns bringing out refreshment from their convent and of being rested and fed when, utterly exhausted, the drivers sank back at their wheels during their weary journey back to Bournemouth.

Exeter, another Police Brigade, and itself an innocent Baedeker-raid city, was crushed and set alight on 3 May 1941. Crews moved in from an assembly point at Starcross and another at Belmont Park. Ted Elgar's crew stopped repeatedly to deal with incendiaries en route to the City centre. Dick Law, in charge of crews, found the big stores and the Centre generally well bombed and burning. He worked on a relay from the river, which was much facilitated by a steel pipe line which fed dams with an unlimited water supply.

He tells of a morning-after incident, when he was approached by a bank manager who, having scrambled his way through the rubbled street, enquired if he could check his safe deposits. Having conducted him through what appeared to be his ruined establishment, they were able to climb below to find the basement virtually unaffected. A grateful bank later contributed to the Fire Services National Benevolent Fund. Jack Dunkley chuckled as he recalled having Tony Forte as a member of his crew. After their night's work, all being tired and hungry, Tony conducted his mates to his undamaged restaurant and ordered a hearty breakfast for all.

Quite amusing tales are told about the journeys to these towns, including Bristol, where crews also met with similar experiences. Can the reader imagine how these crews, sometimes individually and sometimes in convoy, managed with a complete blackout everywhere, with just narrow-slitted headlights which hardly illuminated the roads before them, and without signposts. Ron Harding went to Bristol and debated somewhere en route as to the correct road to take. The mobile dam went one way and his crew another, but both reached their rendezvous. Jack Dunkley's convoy took a turning at Tolpuddle, and being confronted by a duck pond, had to unhitch pumps and perform an about-turn. Chief Officer Barker attended a number of blitzed towns, including the oil storage tanks at Gosport and Avonmouth where, as one previously experienced in oil fire fighting, he was of considerable assistance.

The lads returned home time and time again tired out, wet and grimy, but with that insistent good humour which somehow pervaded people who had become involved in wartime action. Pumps and vehicles were cleaned up and re-stowed with miles of hose, which, being subject to constant scrub and repair was, thanks to the Marsden Hose Dehydrator which had been purchased in June 1940 and installed in a shed at the Central Fire Station, finally dried during those winter months and returned for service. All the AFS whole-time men were issued with greatcoats in January 1941 and were, in several respects, the envy of other brigades. Especially conspicuous was the undress uniform of our Bournemouth professionals which, particularly in London, not only drew attention by virtue of smart brass-edged peak caps and grenade badges, but which also invited the occasional salute. There was, needless to say, a certain justifiable pride in what had been achieved, much through Chief Officer Barker's initiative and through a great deal of hard work by our team. No wonder certain brigades in the South referred to us as "The Aristocrats".

By the end of 1940, 625 men from Bournemouth had attended the various blitzes, taking with them a total of 83 pumps. So many tales of enthusiasm, dedication and downright heroism could be told of our Bournemouth men, yet so few remain with us after such a passage of time. One can only record but a taste of what our Auxiliary Fire Service, born out of Bournemouth Fire Brigade, did for their Service and for their country. Fortunately, none lost their lives during those most hazardous adventures, and records show but two men injured, both in London. They were Auxiliary Fireman E.Pickering and Auxiliary Fireman F. Osborne.

Yet in the midst of all this activity, entertainment was maintained on the various stations, particularly at the Central Fire Station. A popular double-act was that of "Les and Doc", "Doc" being Doctor H.M.King, whose King Edward School had been evacuated from Southampton, and who was to become a most popular Speaker of the House of Commons. After weeks of often-interrupted rehearsals at the station, we went on the air on the BBC's Forces Programme, in a broadcast on 2 November 1940, announced as from "a fire station somewhere in the South of England". Mr Leslie Bridgmont, well known for so many years at the BBC, presented the programme, which was written and produced by Auxiliary Fireman Harry Carter, a prominent member of the local Little Theatre Club.

Twenty-five of us auxiliaries and professionals took our various parts, and we gave voice to a signature tune entitled *Colours and Bells*, which was written by a very fine musician, Deputy Section Officer Bob Sadler, and referred to in the Press as "an AFS song which was one of the most stirring patriotic numbers we have heard".

It was quite an occasion. Ron Harding's new bride Sally, one of several AFS romances, sang *I'll walk beside you*, perhaps appropriately. Roma Samways, who later married our Arthur Linter, played the accordion, and Harry Carter and Barbara Jane, AFS car owner-driver and daughter of the author of *Jane's Fighting Ships*, added to Cupid's triumphs at the Central Fire Station. Yet more – George Cooper returned from Wembley for long enough to marry Auxiliary Firewoman Maisie Vallance; Pat Davis married Dick Law's sister Vera; Auxiliary Leading Fireman Jack Dunkley married Auxiliary Firewoman Cynthia White.

London burning: warehouse inferno as the docklands are blitzed at Millwall, 7 September 1940 (photograph courtesy of London Fire Service); Bournemouth units helped fight the flames.

'Bomb on bungalow kills boy': 11-year-old Stanley Ricketts happened to be walking home past this unoccupied bungalow in Kingsbere Road, Oakdale, Poole, when it received a direct hit on the evening of 11 October 1940.

OPPOSITE – No.1 Zone, Central Fire Station: Bournemouth's Auxiliary Fire Service ready for action with improvised saloon cars (ladders on roof, trailers at rear) and a converted bus (in the background) acting as a mobile water carrier, September 1940.

The Blitz Assessed

As the blitz era advanced, it was understandable and by no means unreasonable that assessments of the effectiveness or otherwise of the Fire Service in wartime were being made by the Service itself, by the Government, by Parliament and by the Press. Variations in degrees of organisation and efficiency were very apparent. Some fire authorities were manifestly incapable of and even resistant to the requirements of fire-fighting operations which severe air attacks demanded. Lessons were certainly being learned the hard way.

In December 1940, the Home Office circularised all fire authorities, asking them to review their emergency arrangements and for reports and suggestions to be made. In the meantime, senior fire officers were summoned to meetings at their regional headquarters in order to prepare recommendations for the Home Office. A co-ordinated report expressed the urgent need for improvement and reorganisation, which involved many features, ranging from the disposition of appliances and crews, fuel supplies and reinforcement schemes to mobilising and the efficiency of control rooms etc.

Fire Brigade Circular 7a/1941 of 5 February 1941, sent to all fire authorities, emphasised the compelling need for far more readily available water supplies and the Government itself needed no persuasion in proceeding not only to recommend the construction of a great number and variety of dams and other local supplies, but actually to order 100 miles of six-inch steel pipeline, together with joints, bends and valves – it was estimated that every mile needed about 150 components – for urgent delivery to towns up and down the country. Later, in July 1941, the Government was to authorise the expenditure of £4m to further the production of supplementary water supplies.

Peter Dorey, soon to be appointed to the rank of Station Officer, was given the task of organising the water supplies in Bournemouth, and later, as a Company Officer in the National Fire Service, planning the construction and routing of considerable distances of steel pipeline which was to serve so well at least the centre of the town. These six-inch pipes, in 20 feet lengths, or half-lengths and quarter-lengths, were bent and shaped as required by the NFS workshop staff. They were laid on the surface of roads and land for the obvious use of water-relaying and as an alternative to the water mains. Whereas underground mains, mostly of cast-iron, fractured easily, these pipes would withstand much in the way of impact and damage, and when damaged they could be fairly simply replaced. The one most convincing lesson learned from the blitz experience by everyone, including the public at large, was that the greatest danger meted out by enemy air assault was that of fire. Parliament itself was told by the Parliamentary Secretary to the Ministry of Home Security: "The experience of all raids, including our own photographs of what we are doing in Germany, shows that the biggest single problem, when a raid is actually in progress, is the problem of fire".

It was later assessed that ton for ton, incendiaries were four to eight times as effective as high-explosive bombs on residential areas. It was obviously imperative that serious efforts to deal with this menace should not rest only upon the fire service but that they should involve every able man-in-the-street. Back in August 1940, a Clearance of Lofts order had been issued publicly and our Fire Brigade Committee had agreed to provide some degree of enforcement by authorising six professional firemen and twelve AFS officers to carry out inspections. It proved to be a somewhat inadequate process.

No. 5.

PROCEEDURE ON FIRE CALLS.

INVASION - DIV.ORDER 31.

TO OFFICERS ONLY.

"STAND BY" MESSAGE.

On receipt of a message "Stand By - Invasion" from Divisional Headquarters through Sub-Divisions to Stations, all personnel must prepare for immediate action and await further instructions. Working parties must cease and men away from Stations must be recalled immediately. Where practicable, men on leave should also be recalled, and as many part-time personnel as possible report for duty.

The other threat: Divisional Order 31 concerned German invasion 'Proceedure' (sic, showing that poor spelling has always been with us) and instructed a return to base if the enemy landed.

Public involvement

Next came a Fire Watchers Order, issued in September 1940, which required a permanent watch at business premises where more than thirty people were employed, and in the case of large warehouses of more than 50,000 cubic feet capacity. On 15 January 1941, new requirements under the Fire Precautions (Business Premises) Order gave a new impetus to a scheme for sounder fire protection and Station Officer Joe Thackwray, Sub-Officer Ivor Bolt and Sub-Officer Pete Dorey, notwithstanding their other commitments, were appointed inspectors under the Order. This applied to "any premises occupied wholly or partly for the purpose of any business, trade or profession". The local Chamber of Trade had itself sprung into action early in January 1941, organising its members and producing a scheme which divided the town into 22 zones.

The Home Secretary's radio appeal on 31 December 1940 made the point that Fire Watching should be everybody's concern, and coinciding with the Fire Precautions (Business Premises) Order, men between ages 16 and 60 had to register for part-time duty of up to 48 hours per month. In March 1941, a local man was fined £1 for failing to carry out his duty. The emphasis upon local organisation was accepted by the Bournemouth Brigade with the kind of enthusiasm that only Chief Officer Barker and his partner Commandant Harold Benwell could bring to bear.

Public meetings were called and attended by overwhelming numbers of people throughout the months that followed, commencing with an attendance of 500 on 15 February 1941. A committee composed of Messrs Benwell, Barker, S.W. Hobbs (ARP Officer) and Colonel R.J. Mallett (Chief Warden) met early in January, for the purpose of organising a grand voluntary fire-watchers programme which would embrace the whole County Borough. Stirrup pumps were distributed in large numbers. Over 500 had been sold to members of the public by the local ARP administration. Whistles were provided to all street-leaders and wardens. By May, 410 steel helmets were being dispensed and 15,000 more were on order. The scheme included an issue of certificates, and again by May, 5,076 were effected. The Bournemouth Times headline for March 28 1941 proclaimed: "Bournemouth has over 17,000 civilian firefighters".

But all of these Government orders did not add up to a satisfactory situation nationally, and in August, with the newly-titled Fire Guard organisation now under the sole control of the ARP, the Home Secretary decided that the scheme could not be left to volunteers. The outcome was the Civil Defence (Compulsory Enrolment) Order 1941, under which all men between the ages of 18 and 60 had to register for fire-guard duties. Registration took place on 14, 20 and 21 September 1941. Those exempted included Home Guards, members of the Armed Forces, members of the Royal Observer Corps, police, doctors, masters and crews of sea-going ships, the registered blind and mentally handicapped. Others, such as members of the Fire Service, had to register but were automatically exempted.

With the pressure, not only of organisation but of the Brigade's exhausting administration, the Fire Brigade Emergency Committee appointed a Fire Prevention clerk (Mr S.J. Alderton) and two typists on 10 February 1941. Sub-Officer Ivor Bolt and Staff Fireman Len Bailey proceeded thereafter to conduct inspections of business premises and to carry out drills. On 15 May, Ivor Bolt was promoted to the rank of Station Officer and Len Bailey to that of Sub-Officer.

Meanwhile the Luftwaffe spared Bournemouth during January and February 1941, though we heard its drone when Cardiff (2 January) and Bristol (3 January) were pounded and Swansea was bombed on three nights (20-22 February). But on 11 March, at 21.08 hours, four high-explosive bombs descended on Throop, causing very little damage, with four more in the Broadway and Yeomans Road area just over an hour later. During the rest of March, there were nine raids with 15 high-explosive bombs dropped, which killed two people, injured 22 and damaged a total of 881 properties at Portland Road, Murley Road, Ripon Road, Hillcrest Road, Gerald Road, Grafton Road, Iddesleigh Road, Queens Road, Surrey Road, Wimborne Road (one bomb on the cemetery), Leven Avenue, Meyrick Park Golf Links, Lowther Road and Methuen Road. Two unexploded bombs in Alma Road necessitated a temporary evacuation of the area. Two water mains were fractured. On 27 March, a direct hit on Bourne Valley Gas Works resulted in the deaths of 33 people.

Carnage at Branksome: a lunchtime bomb on 27 March 1941 hit the canteen at Bourne Valley Gasworks, killing 34 and leaving 23 wounded for ARP wardens and Royal Artillerymen to drag out of the debris (three of the dead were members of the Home Guard).

OPPOSITE – 'Street Fire Fighting Parties': practical advice on do-it-yourself neighbourhood fire precautions, with special emphasis on 'Dealing with incendiary bombs AT ONCE', issued in 1941.

STREET
FIRE FIGHTING
PARTIES

HOUSEHOLDERS :

Every group of five to ten houses should have its Fire Party.

Each street should have a leader.

Each leader should have a board outside his or her house to give notice of any meetings, etc.

DUTIES : BEFORE AN " ALERT "

Organising of Street Parties, for every 30 houses.

Arrangements for each Party to assemble.

Training of parties by A.F.S. and Wardens.

See that each house has plenty of half-filled sandbags outside as well as inside.

See that outside each house as well as inside there are receptacles full of water.

See that each house has landings, passages and lofts clear.

See, wherever possible, ladders are by lofts.

Securing of Stirrup Pumps either from local Council or by a mutual levy of members.

Rota of duties during an " Alert."

Knowledge of nearest hydrants.

Knowledge of nearest Fire Station.

Knowledge of nearest Wardens' Post.

DURING AN " ALERT "

Watchers on duty.

Rota of individual members of Fire Parties on Duty.

Calling on Parties when incendiary bombs fall.

Dealing with incendiary bombs AT ONCE.

FORM YOUR FIRE PARTIES NOW—DON'T WAIT

More bombs on Bournemouth

A memorable night was that of 10 April 1941. First, at 22.14 hours, a single high-explosive bomb was dropped on Westminster Road, causing no damage. Then at 23.57 hours, the Luftwaffe decided to attack both Poole and the centre of Bournemouth. Woolworths, in the Square (now Boots), suffered two direct hits, setting the whole ablaze. As the call came through, a request from Poole for our Turntable Ladders to be sent to the Branksome Towers Hotel was responded to and Chief Officer Barker had to demand its return to Bournemouth Square as soon as he saw our local problem. Off-duty professionals Dick Law and Bill Godwin rushed into Central's appliance room, donned their kit and just caught the Leyland Dual-Purpose appliance. Dick Law relates: "When we arrived we saw Woolworths store well alight. AFS crews were running out hose, and fortunately the hydrants were good and water was plentiful. As the Turntable Ladders arrived, I tried to get the job of operating the monitor, but Pat Davis got there first. Other jets were directed from adjoining roofs and from the road. On orders from the Chief, I grabbed two AFS crews and entered the adjoining premises of Burtons, the tailors, where the fire was bursting through. We saved that shop, in fact all the surrounding property was saved. This was my first local major wartime fire, and like the rest of us young pros.,I confess to enjoying the experience."

In the same raid, other high-explosive bombs fell on Hampshire Court, demolishing three flats and fracturing two water mains; four flats were demolished in St Stephens Road, where a gallant rescue of a woman took place, and other damage affected Richmond Hill Drive and Richmond Hill Gardens. An unexploded bomb was reported in Bodorgan Road. In all, one man and seven women were killed and a total of 112 premises were damaged.

Two nights later, on 12 April at 22.30 hours, more high-explosive bombs were dropped in the vicinity of Bournemouth Square, in the Lower Gardens, the gardens of the Royal Exeter Hotel, on Rotherfell Court and in Bodorgan Road, damaging 42 properties and fracturing a water main. Amazingly there were no casualties. Then, on 16 April at 00.35 hours, five high-explosive bombs were dropped on Kinson, damaging 83 properties in Millhams Lane, Glendon Avenue, Bramley Road and Weymans Avenue.

Two raids occurred in May, the first on the 10th at 00.45

hours, involving parachutes with canisters, which were found in R.L. Stevenson Avenue, Fernside Road, The Avenue and Strathmore Road, where no damage was sustained. The other raid involved one high-explosive bomb and a number of incendiaries which were dropped on Northbourne Avenue at 03.32 hours on 12 May. This was to be the last bombing incident in the life of the Bournemouth Fire Brigade and its Auxiliary Fire Service within our own town.

Many are the tales which abounded. After an incendiary bomb raid, a 16-year-old boy was asked, "And how many have you put out?" He replied, "Well sir, nine altogether, three belonging to those across the road and six of our own."

Chimney fires at night were something of a menace. On one occasion a crew turned out from San Remo Towers (Zone 2) to such an incident at Wharncliffe Mansions, Boscombe. Jerry was overhead and sparks were flying out of the chimney pot. To the amusement of his crew and the chagrin of the stores officer, the AFS Leading Fireman promptly climbed his ladder and placed his tin hat firmly on top of the chimney.

AFS men were increasingly allowed to carry out the functions of the staff firemen. A few who were eligible acted as assistants on ambulance duties. The tale is told of a driver who, half-asleep, slid down the pole at the Central Fire Station, leapt into his seat and drove his appliance straight across Holdenhurst Road into a shop window opposite.

A reminiscent ex-firewoman recalled an incident at Zone 9 (Meyrick Park) station. The crews had their meals at the Sports Pavilion, across the main park. It was night when Jerry hovered overhead and the searchlight crew stationed in the park were on target. Burst after burst of machine-gun fire spattered down the beam and the fire crew had some difficulty in returning to their appliance.

Ready for action: crews from Bournemouth and Portsmouth during the city's blitz, March 1941; on standby outside the Portland House, Fareham.

OPPOSITE – Ready for fun: 'We don't want to set the world on FIRE' on the cover of a programme that promises 'The Dancing Firebelles', Pat and Phil arguing about conjuring, 'The Divisional Male Voice Choir', Sylvia Pratt dancing with distinction, Jimmy Yetman as 'Our Baritone', Nellie Pearmain 'Practically a Lady', and for the finale, 'Knock Off and Make Up'.

NATIONAL FIRE SERVICE

This is a = = =

16c *Divisional*

Entertainment Unit

Programme

Proceeds in aid of
N.F.S. CHARITIES

'Proto': Basil Stocks instructs NFS firemen Dave Ott and George Huxtep ('Echo' reporter) in the one-hour oxygen breathing apparatus.

OPPOSITE – blindfolded: to give 'Proto' training a sense of realism.

More orders: to proceed without deviation, 1942.

No. 5.

PROCEEDURE ON FIRE CALLS.

ENEMY ACTION.

On receipt of a Fire Call <u>one unit</u> is dispatched immediately from the Station. The type of unit sent is at the discretion of the Officer in charge or Mobilising Officer, according to the type of premises involved. Sub-Divisional Control is immediately informed by the usual standard message, plus . any special observations, i.e. Building of National Importance. Pumps <u>MUST</u> proceed to the address to which they are ordered and not stop on the way to deal with any unattended fires.

OVERLEAF – National Fire Service personnel: officers of station 16-C (Bournemouth), No.1 Zone (Central Fire Station, pictured in the yard), in 1942.

End of the old Brigade

The logical outcome of the "grand reassessment" early in 1941 was a recognition of the unreliability of the constitution of the British Fire Service as it then existed. Effective fire protection for the whole country was being somewhat obstructed by the fact that over 1,600 local authorities were functioning independently and a piecemeal situation existed. Regionalisation was discussed, in an endeavour to pacify those who opposed governmental direction, but that was not the answer. Indeed it was considered that it would cause further complications. The complete nationalisation of the Service was the only answer in order to rationalise every facet, including training, ranks, mobilisation, administration and uniform. In fact it was known that Germany itself had moved from local control and adopted this measure.

It was at a very late sitting, on 28 April 1941, that Home Secretary Herbert Morrison, Sir George Gater, Permanent Under-Secretary to the Ministry of Home Security, Sir Arthur Dixon, Assistant Under-Secretary in charge of the Fire Brigades Division of the Home Office, and Commander Firebrace of the London Fire Brigade made their decision to nationalise. This was conveyed to the regional commissioners the following morning.

The War Cabinet approved the plan on 8 May, the local authorities were informed on 10-12 May, the Fire Services (Emergency Provisions) Bill received its second reading on 20 May, and the Bill became an Act of Parliament on 22 May. Or so it was assumed, for in the middle of 1944, it was discovered that it had not been ratified by Parliament!

In Bournemouth those three remarkable and challenging years, 1938-41, revealed the acumen and agility of Chief Officer Barker which, with equally tireless backing, reflected itself in the creation of a most creditable Auxiliary Fire Service. Yet a very sad and regrettable situation had arisen after his arrival in 1938, and worsened as the months proceeded especially within the confines of the Brigade's sanctum. Ambivalence somewhat inevitably descended without much hesitation between Ken Devereux, the Deputy Chief Officer and the new Chief who, with some hauteur and condescension – his bearing, with hands at right-angles, caused some amusement – presumed us to be something of a yokel fire brigade. We were all faced with an entirely new situation and we were not unnaturally shaken at the sudden abandonment of an established and agreeable atmosphere in which we had worked for so long.

The introduction of a master, rightly self-willed yet dominantly producing not merely new ideas but an entirely new philosophy, was disconcerting. Some of us, at least, were under few illusions, in the spring of 1938, as to the considerable task ahead, but we were to feel that an atmosphere of intolerance could only serve to aggravate, as indeed it did. Ken Devereux had worked extremely hard for many years with the sense of dedication, the high degree of adaptability, and the acceptance of team-work of which we were all proud. To find himself virtually ordered into subservience was too much for the normally quiet and inoffensive Deputy Chief.

In consequence Ken Devereux underwent constant humiliation and his standing was so undermined that he eventually found himself subordinated into carrying out elementary tasks such as keeping the fire occurrence log book. A feeling of inexpediency was reflected throughout the Brigade and beyond. The Chief's demand for his fuel to be carried up to his flat was at first refused by several men. Mr Barker was not "our favourite uncle".

The situation was not helped by his London method of "drowning" fires, as illustrated by an occurrence at 11.06 pm on 1 August 1938 at Butley Dene, a large house in Christchurch Road, near St Swithuns Road. Roof timbers were well aglow, but flame had not broken through to the open air. Ken Devereux and I were quite satisfactorily dealing with the situation with two hose reels, when the Chief arrived and called for several lengths of hose, 525 feet in all. A main jet in the roof blew off the slates, the fire roared and the whole house was so devastated with water that the plaster fell from the walls and the house had to be demolished. Our reaction was unprintable.

On 14 February 1939, a fire at the Lever Galleries in Westover Road resulted in knee-deep water in the basement and the use of two light trailer pumps to extract it. This was a peace-time fire-fighting procedure which was quite foreign to us.

After a year had passed, during which time the Deputy Chief had been acting as an AFS instructor, the aggravation was such that it could not be ignored by the Fire Brigade Committee. Its secret meeting was not minuted or reported to the Council, but nevertheless, it became known and caused a furore at the March 1939 Council meeting. Councillor Langton observed: "We should be advised from a proper source what is taking place and not be left to pick up information on public service vehicles and in the streets." The Press remarked: "The secrecy has defeated its own object, because these differences and the manner of settling them are being freely talked about in the town with an increasing amount of inaccuracy we suppose." Despite discussions between the Deputy Chief and the Town Clerk, which were reported to the Fire Brigade Committee on 13 June 1940, and again on 11 October 1940, the situation remained unchanged. At the Council meeting of 1 April 1941, questions were asked as to why the Deputy Chief was not in charge at the Central Fire Station whilst the Chief was away answering blitz calls.

On 15 April 1941 a further special meeting of the Committee was held at which I appeared as a witness. By this time, a situation had arisen which caused such distress amongst both the professionals and the AFS that Sub-Officer Dorey called a meeting of the former on 27 April, after which the AFS section leaders met the following day. The following month, Ken Devereux was ordered to vacate his flat at the Central Fire Station and to move, with Muriel, his invalid wife, to temporary accommodation in Winton, in order that he should "take over" that area. For many months, I repeatedly typed applications for posts in other brigades on his behalf, but despite the fact that in 1938, he had been duly hoodwinked and initiated into the First Degree of Freemasonry — and how thrilled he was — he considered himself, by virtue of more senior intervention, to have been blackballed. Eventually, on 9 July 1941, he left to take up a post as Co-ordinating Officer at Hartford in Cheshire, and tragically, it was the end of his career.

As for myself, being involved and otherwise observing all matters relating to the Brigade administration, life was, to say the least, disenchanting. There existed, within the close confines of our two offices, a philosophical divergence which in no way could be compounded. I registered for duty with the Royal Navy on 27 April 1941, only to be refused release by Chief Officer Barker. On 29 April 1941, with internal conditions deteriorating, I had two private meetings with the Town Clerk and further meetings with Councillor Dr Lyster, and with Canon Hedley Burrows on the following day. Early in June, the Fire Brigade Committee met to consider certain allegations which were being aimed at the Chief Officer. Having been warned of my impending presence once again as a witness, I duly received my Chief's vigorous commination on 31 May 1941.

On 15 May 1941, Home Office Fire Brigade Circular 39/41 announced the forthcoming nationalisation of the Service. Chief

Officer William Howard Barker, M.I.Fire E, A.F.A.R.P.I. (Associate Fellow of the Air Raid Protection Institute), received notification of his appointment as Fire Force Commander of No 15 Area (Berks, Bucks and Oxon) from 21 July, at a salary of £900 per annum. Hearing this, the Committee granted him a month's pay in lieu of two years' disregarded annual leave. At a gathering on 22 July he was presented with a table lamp by some of the AFS personnel and a gold watch by Commandant (Councillor) Benwell. Rather aptly, Councillor Thomson remarked that he was a "Barker, but could also bite".

On 28 July 1941, F.F.C. Barker left for Area Headquarters at Taplow, Buckinghamshire, taking with him Ernest Woodrow as his NFS Area Clerk. Ivor Bolt left to join him on 23 August, and Len Bailey likewise on 8 September. Upon the Chief's departure, Station Officer Thackwray was appointed Acting Officer-in-Charge, with Ivor Bolt as his Deputy. As for the administration, the whole rested upon me until that most fateful of days, 18 August 1941, when the Bournemouth Fire Brigade ceased to exist, as did its clerkship.

So it was farewell to Chief Officer Barker who, let it be said, was "a man of his time". He was a wartime fire service leader who happened on Bournemouth and produced a model auxiliary fire service through foresight and considerable energy. His sense of authority in all quarters was such that even Bournemouth Council bowed to his demands. With the Chairman of the Fire Brigade Committee as his "No.1", his passage was always clear. It takes a war to produce wartime leadership – peace is another state of being.

With Mr Barker at least temporarily esconced at "White Place", Taplow – he left for a further appointment after a few months – just one or two skeletal bones fell into the Bournemouth Council Chamber on 7 October 1941. The Bournemouth Times blazoned "Stormy Council debate about Fire Brigade affairs – Former Chief Officer alleged to be involved." Matters concerning AFS food and a car which belonged to a certain reverend gentleman emerged. The Echo reported on 9 October 1941, "Councillor Scott in a lengthy speech gave an account of the manufacture by firemen of a household staircase in the carpenters' shop at the Central Fire Station, and repairs by Bournemouth firemen to a boat on the river at Christchurch." But William Howard Barker must be remembered in Bournemouth as a quite outstanding organiser of a fire brigade and the vital needs of war which, without doubt, outshone other brigades throughout the country. Difficult to keep up with indeed, but a leader when leadership was so needed. Eventually he was appointed Chief Fire Officer of Devon on the return to local authority control in 1948.

As has been suggested, the formation of the National Fire Service was as necessary as it was inevitable, for it was a question not only of nationalisation but also of rationalisation. Although the Auxiliary Fire Service had worked generally with much satisfaction during the great blitz period, thanks mainly to the guts and good temper of the men who manned the pumps under the most frightful conditions, and drove that extraordinary variety of vehicles, the future of the war and the prospect of more furious and sustained bombardment was still very much a possibility. Yet it was so regrettable that a number of fire authorities, including some who themselves suffered blitz conditions, failed to organise properly or adjust themselves to all the stages through which the Government had endeavoured to conduct them.

In Bournemouth our Auxiliary Fire Service was in a healthy condition, and the final roll-call showed the following:

	Whole-time	Part-time	Total
Men	340	250	590
Women	18	110	128
Car Owner Drivers	Nil	45	45
Messengers	20	165	185
			948

NFS: badge of the National Fire Service, 1941-48.

The National Fire Service

It is not my intention to depart much from the era of the Bournemouth Fire Brigade or to enter into the realms of the National Fire Service, which took over from 18 August 1941 until 31 March 1948, a period of impermanence and perhaps a little unreality. Of course, there were many positive features, particularly where national, regional and area relationships were concerned, and in improvements of equipment, pumps, towing vehicles (purpose-built Austin vans replaced the assortment of cars and lorries) and water supplies. The standardisation of training was an essential asset, and in connection with this there appeared in 1942 the first of a series of well-produced *Manuals of Firemanship*.

National Fire Service drill books were soon in evidence. Useful no doubt where less initiative had been used in training procedures, it contained such performances as "Saluting" and "Wheel-changing to numbers". For example: "On the order 'Change wheel', No 1 proceeds to the nearest telephone, No 2 provides jack and lever and lifts appliance, No 3 provides wheel-brace and loosens nuts, No 4 puts down chocks and removes spare wheel." And so on.

We were introduced to drills for ceremonial occasions, including "Off Helmets", "Three Cheers For ..." and similar indispensibles. With new and often unhabituated people shouting orders, Bournemouth's professional firemen were not impressed and indeed a degree of humiliation was not unknown.

Inevitably, there appeared to be more officers than men. The operational pyramid was based on a crew of five men. A Leading Fireman had charge of one crew, a Section Leader had charge of five, a Company Officer had charge of ten and a Column Officer had charge of fifty crews, all with their pumps, of course. A Divisional Officer officially was in charge of 100 pumps and crews, although he had charge of the administration of his division. Above the Division we had the Fire Force Commander with his staff, and at regional headquarters the Chief Regional Fire Officer and his grand retinue. No 6 Region covered East Hampshire, including Portsmouth and the Isle of Wight (Area 14 − F.F.C. Charters); Berkshire, Buckinghamshire and Oxfordshire (Area 15 − F.F.C. Barker followed by F.F.C. Taylor); the remainder of Hampshire and part of Dorset (Area 16 − F.F.C. Hayward followed by F.F.C. Paramor).

Area 16 of No 6 Region had three divisions with headquarters at Southampton (16.A), Kingsworthy (16.B) and Bournemouth (16.C). Divisional Officer Stanley Fairbrass, ex-Chief Officer of Cowes and a Dagenham colleague and friend of W.H.Barker, arrived at the Central Fire Station, Holdenhurst Road, on 25 August 1941.

NFS administration was conducted by a hierarchy of officers, their deputies and their female staffs, a structure repeated at divisional level, area level and regional level. Each comprised a Chief Clerk, a Finance Officer, an Establishment Officer, a Transport Officer, an Accommodation Officer, a Water Officer, a Stores Officer, a Catering Officer and a Mobilising Officer. I was left wondering how I and Ernest Woodrow possibly managed during the far more difficult pre-NFS period!

As far as original appointments and ranks were concerned in the NFS, it was certainly difficult for professional firemen, in particular, to comprehend the significance of the complete change-over which faced them on 18 August 1941. Legally, as it were, everyone on that fateful day was thrown into the melting pot, and reverted, irrespective of previous position or service, to the rank of fireman. How bewildering it was to be expected to salute people who so recently had been newcomers and auxiliary trainees. It was disconcerting, to say the least, to see so many officers who were, often enough, associated with local business. I found my desk so occupied on that morning by a newly-uniformed Divisional Clerk who, quite unapologetically, confirmed his authority. Like a flash, it was the end of a long career. There was some sense of urgency in the need of former chief fire officers and their friends to effect officer appointments before the Appointed Day, but the air of secrecy which pervaded the once-happy Central Fire Station created a blot which was never quite erased. Some new officers came from other towns, and what better place to settle than Bournemouth, where sea-bathing was again allowed as from 12 July 1941. Good humour prevailed, notwithstanding the drastic changes, and often enough, the mickey was taken out of the new and inexperienced glove-carrying gentlemen. One recalls persuading a company officer to fill his cigarette-lighter with carbon-tetrachloride, which was once used in hand fire extinguishers.

NEXT PAGES – Beales burns and the Hotel Metropole is destroyed: 77 civilians died and more than a hundred Canadian airmen, gathered for Sunday lunch in the Hotel Metropole beside the Lansdowne roundabout, as sixteen Focke-Wulf 190s swept in from the sea in a daylight bombing raid, 23 May 1943.

Emergency reservoir: surface storage tank, 1942.

Emergency pipeline: 6 inch pipe in the gutter on the corner of Hinton Road and Gervis Place, beside J.E. Beale Limited's department store (which would be blitzed on 23 May 1943), providing an easily repairable surface supply of water for town centre fire fighting, 1942.

Bobby's blitzed: drapers Bobby and Co. Limited, the Square, Bournemouth, with severe blast damage – but spared from fire – after the Focke-Wulf 190s devastated the town centre, 23 May 1943.

PREVIOUS PAGES – Fire-fighting and rescue: saving Beales was a lost cause and its clock crashed into Old Christchurch Road, but a turntable ladder brought out some Canadian airmen alive from the rubble of the Hotel Metropole, on the afternoon of 23 May 1943.

Local N.F.S. in action – the Sunday Blitz

The prayer of the Bournemouth Fire Brigade was that, with a grand victory for those fighting lads in Europe, we would find eventual satisfaction from the assurance which Herbert Morrison gave to the House of Commons on 20 May 1941: "I will give this House this assurance, which I gave to the local authorities last week. It is the very definite intention of the Government that this is a wartime expedient only, produced by war conditions, made necessary by a battle, an active fight that is going on day by day. It is certainly my very definite view that, after the war, the fire-fighting forces should again be a local authority service, that is to say that they should not be permanently run by the State, but should again become a local authority service."

Local bombing by the Luftwaffe continued at intervals for almost three years of the NFS. The first did not occur until 7 October 1941 at 21.20 hours, when two parachute mines were dropped on the Pier Approach and the East Beach, into the sea. These smashed windows in Bath Road, including the Royal Bath Hotel and "Rothesay", Westover Road, Old Christchurch Road and the East Beach café and office. Two people sustained cuts from flying glass and 235 properties were affected.

All was quiet until 25 May 1942, when two raids, at 00.15 and 01.00 hours, took place, The first involved a delayed action high-explosive bomb and one large bomb which produced a crater in the Upper Pleasure Gardens 55 feet by 63 feet by 15 feet deep. Its blast smashed a 42 inch storm sewer and damaged 141 properties, including the town hall, Fairlight Glen and a large number of shops and flats. The second raid, three-quarters of an hour later, involved four high-explosives producing craters 15 feet deep,one 35 feet and the other 30 feet in diameter, on a tennis court, bowling green and on the cliffs. These damaged 22 premises. On 28 May 1942, the delayed action bomb, implanted three days previously, exploded in the Upper Pleasure Gardens, near the war memorial, and closed Avenue Road and Bourne Avenue. On 6 June 1942, high-explosive bombs were dropped near St Peter's Church, on the Anglo-Swiss Hotel, on Hill House in Parsonage Road and on a railway siding in Southcote Road, damaging a total of 454 properties.

The unforgettable Sunday was 23 May 1943, when at 13.00 hours, about two dozen Focke-Wulf fighter-bombers and Me109 fighters dived upon our sunny seaside town. Bombs fell on Upper Terrace Road, Bobbys in The Square, Exeter Road, the Central Hotel and the old Punshon Memorial Church (opened by Rev W. Morley on 30 June 1886), on Richmond Hill, the Shamrock and Rambler Garage in Holdenhurst Road, the Metropole Hotel at the Lansdowne, West's Cinema (now the Burlington Arcade), Beales in Old Christchurch Road, Lansdowne Road, Queens Park South Drive, Richmond Wood Road, Howeth Road, Drummond Road, Manor Road, Vale Road, Bethia Road, Spring Road, 248 Holdenhurst Road, Cotlands Road and Dean Park Road. 77 men, women and children were killed (excluding a number of airmen at the Metropole Hotel) and 196 were injured. A man was also killed later whilst demolishing Beales. 3,481 premises were affected. One bomber, with bomb intact, crashed in Grove Road.

Another later crashed into the sea after bursts from a triple-mounted Lewis gun fired by Lance-Bombadier Norman Lawrence and Lance-Bombadier John Howard of the Light Anti-Aircraft Regiment, Royal Artillery. Norman recalls "the sound of planes, and low over the sea came three German fighters, machine guns and cannons blazing". John vividly remembers "the enemy aircraft coming at us. It almost seemed as if I and the pilots were looking into each other's eyes, they were that low: just over roof-top height. We opened fire and I am sure I helped to save bloodshed in the Central Gardens, as they climbed quickly. The [incendiary bomb] crater incidentally was just five yards from my position. It was a miracle that I was unharmed as bullets were passing all around me."

Both Norman and John received the B.E.M. in recognition of their heroic rescue of their colleagues (and their guns), who they carried down Beales's spiral staircase. A further thought from John: "I often wonder what happened to the young lady who only minutes beforehand had come out to sunbathe on a rooftop some two hundred yards away." C'est la guerre!

Arthur Linter, a Bournemouth professional fireman appointed to the rank of company officer, writes: "It was a typical wartime Sunday midday in the town centre, when the atmosphere was rudely shattered by the sound of low-flying aircraft and gunfire. They appeared over the Square from the direction of the English Channel, coming in at sea level to escape detection by radar. From the fire escape staircase of my flat at the top of Commercial Road, I saw several planes, one passing immediately overhead and swooping right towards the town centre. A number of loud explosions followed and clouds of dust and smoke could be seen in various parts. Through the gaps in the smoke, I could see what appeared to be a large incident in the vicinity of Bournemouth Square developing.

"As previously arranged, though off duty, I immediately reported to the West Hill Fire Station, where I collected a crew of part-time NFS personnel, the whole-time crews having already left. We proceeded down towards the town centre where a horrific sight confronted us. There were a number of persons lying either injured or worse at various points, and fires raging all around. My crew and myself drove our appliance up Old Christchurch Road towards Beales, but just as we were approaching the Bournemouth Arcade, our way was blocked.

"I proceeded on foot and I was fortunate to encounter Fire Force Commander Hayward who, by chance, had been attending a large fire exercise locally. He ordered me to get a message to our Fire Control, requesting twelve pumps to attend the major incident at and around Beales, which had received a direct hit and was well alight, the fire being fed by gas escaping from a fractured main. The extent and severity of this raid became more apparent, with major incidents in Exeter Road, Holdenhurst Road, The Lansdowne and Richmond Hill. In addition, the West's Picture House was hit, with fire resulting. Several buildings in this vicinity had smaller outbreaks of fire in upper floors, due to burning embers from the larger fires blowing in the hot atmosphere. These were successfully dealt with by the NFS trained stirrup-pump parties, and they certainly did a good job."

Arthur paid tribute to the Salvation Army and others who provided hot drinks and refreshment. Ken Brocklesby narrowly missed being hit by Beales's large clock as it fell to the ground. Dick Law writes: "It was about 1300 hours on a nice quiet Sunday. The sun was shining and it was a warm pleasant day, but not for long. I was in the watchroom, looking out of the window of the NFS Hillview Road Fire Station. Someone said "Bloody hell, Jerries!" We then saw two clouds of smoke go up as they hit somewhere in the town. It was only a few minutes after when the bells went down and we were ordered to the Shamrock and Rambler Coach Station in Holdenhurst Road. As we approached it was devastation all around, but not much fire.

"A company officer stopped me and told me to proceed, with my pumps to Beales. It had been hit and was on fire. As I proceeded past Cotlands Road, I saw to my horror that the fire service flats had been hit, and mine, at No 4, had all the windows out and the front door damaged. I wondered how my wife and her sister were. Were they alive? I couldn't stop but had to go on. However someone got a message to me that the girls were OK and were helping at the Metropole Hotel, a few yards away, which had received a direct hit when it was full of Canadian airmen.

"Fortunately there was no fire, but many airmen (35 in fact) had to be rescued, some from the upper floors, where the new 100 feet Turntable Ladders were put to good use. When we reached Beales, it was well alight and severely damaged. Debris was all across the road. The immediate job was to attempt to contain the fire.

"Forward planning by Pete Dorey, in charge of emergency water supplies, proved to be extremely valuable, as his six-inch steel pipeline was tried and tested. Light pumps were set in on prepared concrete hard standing and pumped thousands of gallons of water, thanks to the damming of the stream in the Upper Gardens. It all worked as Pete said that it would. Canvas dams were set up around the building, each containing 500 gallons of water, and in spite of a huge demand for water by our pumps, they were brimming full all through the action. We even had a second supply ready to hand into the system from the river at Redhill.

"It was said that we could have floated Beales out to sea. I could not get near to get effective jets near the building because of the heat, but as my orders were to try to hold it from the nearby Arcade, I took crews up on the roof of the shops at the rear of Beales in Gervis Place. There I was able to place branch-men with one-inch jets directed across the road, straight into the upper floors. Another crew were playing jets into windows where Beales adjoins the Arcade, which proved successful. Once I had established this, I went into the street, which was running with water and filled with debris and tangled lines of hose. I put another crew to work with two fire-stream director sets, using the impinging-jet principle, with which I had so often drilled my crews. This system involves two one-inch jets being directed to hit one another, resulting in a huge water-curtain. In this way, we protected shops like J.J. Allens in The Quadrant and Lawleys in Old Christchurch Road which might well have been set alight by heat radiation as paintwork had been blistered. Fire Force Commander Hayward was present and five pumps surrounded the building. There is no doubt that, by virtue of the plentiful supply of men, pumps and water, the Beales fire was contained and central Bournemouth was saved from what could have been a disaster of some magnitude."

Prudently conceived were the drills carried out in March 1941 when water relays were put into operation from the Bourne

Stream through the length of Old Christchurch Road.

The Metropole Hotel rescue operation was interesting because of the methods used. With the side of the building blown out, the trapped and injured airmen were strapped to fire service stretchers and small ladders and lowered by line from the Turntable Ladders, operated by Fireman Roger Dehon. His crew consisted of Leading Fireman Griffiths (a well-known local schoolteacher), Fireman Miles, Fireman Northover, Fireman Smith and Fireman Pearce. They rescued thirty or more men. Such stretcher rescue procedure was a drill exercise in the Brigade for many pre-war years.

Eddie Robichaud, a 21-year-old Canadian airman at the time, describes the scene at the Metropole: "I'd gone up to see one of the corporals on the fourth floor at lunchtime. That was when the first bomb hit. Everything went dusty, then the second bomb hit and blew shut the door of the bedroom we were in. We waited for the dust to settle and saw the window had been blown out and was blocked up with bricks. I looked up at the wall and I could see bodies crunched up in the chimney. We just kept shouting for a while and they got us out at about 4 o'clock." Eddie was trapped in the room with three comrades before firemen managed to dig the floor away to rescue them.

Another important factor of the incident was that the absence of fire was to the credit of the boilerman, Mr David Geear, who, despite being himself at risk, had the presence of mind to close down the fires and to switch off all electrical power. Despite much falling debris he forced his way to the power switches, the blast from the bomb having brought down two huge staircases in front of his boiler room. He was later honoured by the Canadian Commander, who presented him on parade with an award of the Three Silver Oak Leaves. He was also "Commended for brave conduct in Civil Defence" by Winston Churchill, his name appearing in the London Gazette.

The hotel proprietor owed his life to the fact that he was standing on the steps outside the hotel. Later his wife's body was brought out. Another woman was eventually rescued after being buried for nineteen hours.

On 12 August 1943 at 01.10 hours, eight high-explosives were dropped at the junction of Firs Glen Road and Woods View Road, the junction of Wilton and Gloucester Roads (setting gas mains alight), the junction of Boundary and Beswick Roads, Spring Road (burst water main), Shelbourne Road and Charminster Avenue. Thirteen people were killed and 21 injured. 1,455 properties were damaged.

On 1 November 1943 at 17.45 hours, 23 high-explosives were dropped on the junction of Heron Court Road and Gerald Road, at the junction of Cecil Avenue and Howard Road, Queens Park Avenue (on the golf links), Campbell Road, Borthwick Road, Avon Road, Chatsworth Road, Bennett Road, Orcheston Road, Shaftesbury Road and Shelbourne Road. One person was killed and 27 injured; and 1,284 properties were damaged.

Phosphorus and incendiary bombs rained down on 24 April 1944 at 02.17 hours and landed at the junction of Stour Road and Avon Road area and at Gresham Road. In addition, an unexploded bomb accompanied incendiaries at Strouden Road, and there were incendiaries at Beatty Road, Portland Road, Shelbourne Road, Holdenhurst Road, Charminster Road, Malvern Road and West Way. Two people were killed, seven injured and 156 properties were damaged. A number of fires kept the NFS lads busy.

The last bombs to fall on Bournemouth were a batch of incendiaries which hit the Roxy Cinema in Holdenhurst Road, and a number of premises nearby, on 27 May 1944.

Snakes of hoses: from the Bourne stream, in the Lower Pleasure Gardens, to fight the fire at Beales, 23 May 1943.

The final scene

The National Fire Service extended itself, over its first few months, to a total of 100,000 men, although reductions took place and the figure was 31,000 by the end of 1945. Munificent form-filling gladdened the hearts of at least those of "Yes Minister" mentality, and a peak of approximately 300 report forms of one kind or another was eventually reached.

Operational highlights of the NFS included "Operation Colour Scheme", when some 9,000 men and 2,000 women descended from the northern half of England into the regions of the south coast, together with 1,240 pumps, being prior to the invasion of Europe (D-Day) on 6 June 1944. The intention was to provide protection for the enormous quantities of war material, ammunition dumps and camps, which were crammed into woods, forests and every convenient spot in the South. Several hundred of our northern colleagues came into Bournemouth and district, requiring much organisation and recognition of dialect. Later, after the Allies became consolidated across the Channel, an "overseas contingent" scheme was devised whereby firemen might accompany the troops, in order to provide fire protection for military equipment and to deal with possible scorched earth tactics by the enemy. Four columns, each with 520 men and 140 pumps, were mobilised from volunteers within the NFS. Several of our local lads joined these columns and participated in the rather robust army-type commando training, including Joe Thackwray, who was a column officer-in-charge, and colleague Dick Law. Three columns were soon disbanded but one went overseas at the request of an American unit, in January 1945.

The last type of air attack on our country, before Jerry fled before our Allied Forces, apart from the butterfly bomb, which exploded on touch, took the form of the Flying Bomb (V1), which first fell on Cuckfield in Sussex, Swanscombe near Gravesend, Platt near Sevenoaks and Bethnal Green on 12-13 June 1944. Three days later on 16 June, 144 of these pilotless aircraft crossed our south-east coast, 73 landing on London. On that same day, our nearest and only such visitor was found by a puzzled local police force in Church Road, Ferndown. Flying at 350 mph, these strange missiles continued to cross our coast until 29 March 1945, in fact a total number of 5,823. 2,420 fell on London and 80 on Hampshire. Then rockets (V2) descended particularly on London out of the blue on 9 September, in fact 517 out of a total of 1,054. Both V1s and V2s carried approximately 2,000 lbs of explosives.

With the last "Red Alert" sounding in England on 29 March 1945, the end of the European war was to follow on 8 May 1945.

The final number of air attacks on major towns, excluding V1s and V2s, read as follows: London 354, Portsmouth 72, Plymouth 71, Southampton 67, Portland 66, Bristol 56, Birmingham 51. The London casualties numbered 80,000, and in the rest of the country there were 146,777. Bournemouth suffered 219 killed and 507 injured.

The estimated tonnage of high-explosive bombs dropped on London was 18,291, on Portsmouth 687, on Southampton 647 and on Bristol 919.

2,272 bombs of various types had been deposited on Bournemouth, destroying 75 properties. 171 required demolition, and a further 13,345 suffered damage from slight to severe. Locally, we received 959 "Red Alerts" and 16 late warnings (after bombs had been dropped), and 59 bombs were dropped without any warning.

The total number of Fire Service casualties in the country included 793 firemen and 25 firewomen killed and 7,000 severely injured. Awards to our Service were two George Crosses, 90 George Medals, 194 British Empire Medals and 395 Commendations.

And so ended the catastrophic Second World War, born once again of supreme idiocy and conquered by guts and guidance. Could the world, much less the British Fire Service, ever return to what was once normality? For nothing in life stands still. Back to local authority control it was for us, as this writer has described elsewhere.

FEL 623: Bournemouth's 100 foot Merryweather turntable ladder – the brigade's first all-steel set – which was delivered in June 1939 and rescued Canadian airmen from the bombed remains of the Hotel Metropole at the Lansdowne, 23 May 1943.

Firewomen: marching through the Bournemouth pines – National Fire Service division 16-C on parade, 1945.

Index

AFS /NFS = Auxiliary later (1941) National Fire Service
BFB = Bournemouth (professional) Fire Brigade